Appetizers &
Hors d'Oe

HALLIE DONNELLY
JANET KESSEL FLETCHER
Writers

SALLY W. SMITH
Editor

LINDA HINRICHS
CAROL KRAMER
Designers

JOEL GLENN
Photographer

CHERIE MILLER
Food Stylist

JAN RHODES
Photographic Stylist

Ortho Books

Publisher
Robert L. Iacopi

Editorial Director
Min S. Yee

Managing Editors
Jim Beley
Anne Coolman
Susan Lammers
Michael D. Smith
Sally W. Smith

Production Director
Ernie S. Tasaki

Editors
Richard H. Bond
Alice E. Mace

System Manager
Christopher Banks

System Consultant
Mark Zielinski

Asst. System Managers
Linda Bouchard
William F. Yusavage

Photographic Director
Alan Copeland

Photographers
Laurie A. Black
Richard A. Christman

Asst. Production Manager
Darcie S. Furlan

Associate Editor
Jill Fox

Production Editors
Don Mosley
Anne Pederson

Chief Copy Editor
Rebecca Pepper

Photo Editors
Kate O'Keeffe
Pam Peirce

National Sales Manager
Charles H. Aydelotte

Sales Associate
Susan B. Boyle

Operations Assistant
Gail L. Davis

Administrative Assistant
Georgiann Wright

Address all inquiries to
Ortho Books
Chevron Chemical Company
Consumer Products Division
575 Market Street
San Francisco, CA 94105

Copyright © 1985
Chevron Chemical Company
All rights reserved under
international and Pan-American
copyright conventions.

First Printing in July, 1985

1 2 3 4 5 6 7 8 9
85 86 87 88 89 90

ISBN 0-89721-055-7

Library of Congress Catalog Card
Number 85-070881

Chevron Chemical Company
575 Market Street, San Francisco, CA 94105

Danielle Walker *(left)* is chairman of the board and founder of the California Culinary Academy. **Hallie Donnelly** *(center)*, a native San Franciscan, has been a chef-caterer for ten years. She holds a degree in music from the University of California, Berkeley, and attended the California Culinary Academy. In France, she studied cooking with Michel Guérard, Roger Vergé, and André Daguin. She has been chef in an executive dining room and on ocean-going sailboats, has frequently catered for California wineries, and has had her own cooking school and television show. The author of a book on sushi and sashimi, she is presently a consultant for hotels and restaurants. **Janet Kessel Fletcher** *(right)* is a free-lance food and wine writer and editor. She holds a degree in economics from Stanford University and attended the Culinary Institute of America in Hyde Park, N.Y. She has cooked in several West Coast restaurants, including the highly acclaimed Chez Panisse, and now writes a weekly restaurant column for the Oakland *Tribune*. In addition, she writes and produces newsletters, brochures, and promotional literature for clients in the food and wine industry.

The California Culinary Academy Among the forefront of American institutions leading the culinary renaissance in this country, the California Culinary Academy in San Francisco has gained a reputation as one of the most outstanding professional chef training schools in the world. With a teaching staff recruited from the best restaurants of western Europe, the California Culinary Academy educates students from around the world in the preparation of classical cuisine. The recipes in this book were created in consultation with the chefs of the California Culinary Academy.

Front Cover
Shrimp with Homemade Cocktail Sauce (see page 51) and Bouchées (see page 82) with chopped Sautéed Red Peppers (see page 36) are among the many delicious recipes you'll find in this book.

Title Page
For a savory appetizer, try Prosciutto and Red Peppers (see page 36) nestled in endive leaves.

Back Cover
Upper Left: Leeks, carrots, potatoes, onions, garlic, and herbs are just some of the ingredients that go into a rich veal stock. This stock can later be used in a variety of ways for everything from soup to sauces.

Upper Right: Trout garnished with lemon and parsley are ready to enter the fish poacher, where they will be simmered in white wine and herbs.

Lower Left: Four Cornish game hens are arranged artfully on a platter with baby carrots and green beans. Among the lessons to be learned from professional chefs is that the way food is presented is just as important as how it tastes.

Lower Right: Rosettes of whipped cream are piped onto a cake with a pastry bag and an open-star tip. As a finishing touch, they add an elegant look to a chocolate cake.

No portion of this book may be reproduced without written permission from the publisher.

We are not responsible for unsolicited manuscripts, photographs, or illustrations.

Every effort has been made at the time of publication to guarantee the accuracy of the names and addresses of information sources and suppliers and in the technical data contained. However, the reader should check for his own assurance and must be responsible for selection and use of suppliers and supplies.

C O N T E N T S

Appetizers &
Hors d'Oeuvres

Flowers, imaginative and beautiful containers for beverages and food, colorful utensils, all help set the stage for entertaining with style.

Hors d'Oeuvres: Overture to the Meal

I t's been said that throwing a party is like staging a Broadway show. And like the overture to a musical, hors d'oeuvres set the tone of the event. This book is filled with imaginative overtures for entertaining. The second, and largest, chapter offers a repertoire of hors d'oeuvres from around the world. The third chapter puts hors d'oeuvres in a party setting, with twelve lively Menus for Entertaining. And this chapter begins at the beginning, with tips from professional party givers (caterers) on selecting and presenting hors d'oeuvres, wine service, and making the most of your pre-party time.

Taking It Literally

When it comes to *hors d'oeuvres*, the French means what it says: outside (*hors*) of the main work (*d'oeuvre*). The hors d'oeuvre is not the main event, but a tempting nibble that precedes it, an *appetizer* that excites, rather than satiates, the appetite. Thus the cardinal rule for pre-dinner hors d'oeuvres is, "Keep it light." A dainty sliver of a warm crab tart will leave guests hungry for more, which is as it should be.

To every rule, however, there are exceptions. In many social circles, a cocktail party or a cocktail buffet is interpreted as more than a prelude to dinner. In many cases, it *is* the dinner. If your guests will be chatting and drinking for two or three hours, they will certainly need some substantial fare. A variety of hors d'oeuvres, abundantly served, will buffer the alcohol and suffice as dinner for many guests. As a general rule, the longer your cocktail "hour" and the harder the liquor, the more generous should be your hors d'oeuvres.

A Balancing Act

Match the food with the mood. The sort of hors d'oeuvres that would be suitable at a backyard barbecue wouldn't tempt an elegant crowd in designer wear. Grilled hors d'oeuvres are great for backyard parties. Try Texas-style Cocktail Ribs (page 54), Indonesian Chicken Skewers (page 63), or Sicilian Pork Skewers with Sage (page 62). The more rustic hors d'oeuvres, like Polenta Tarts with Red Pepper Filling (page 76), Carnitas (page 56), or Roasted Garlic Confit (page 29), somehow seem to taste better outdoors. And anything likely to be messy—Pollo Pequeño (page 56), for example—can be saved for outdoor meals.

For elegant occasions, choose hors d'oeuvres that people don't need to fuss with, like Curried Crab in Tiny Cream Puffs (page 42), Sushi (page 48), or Seven-Onion Cream Tarts (page 80). Save the spreads and dips for more casual occasions, when guests aren't afraid to dig in. To set an easygoing mood, consider Pizza (page 83), Focaccia (page 87), or one of the more unusual meatball dishes (page 60).

Coordinating hors d'oeuvres with one another and with the rest of the meal is just common sense, but many hosts and hostesses overlook this step. If you'll be serving a full-course meal, use the hors d'oeuvres to set the tone. Presenting an elegant seafood mousse before a casual dinner of barbecued ribs confuses the palate and the mood. Serve like with like, both in terms of the cuisine—Italian starters with Italian meals—and in terms of style—elegant starters with elegant meals.

If you're serving several hors d'oeuvres with no meal to follow, the hors d'oeuvres should complement one another. Learn to balance textures and flavors, hot and cold, cooked and raw, simple and hearty. Juxtapose something cold and clean and simple—like marinated vegetables—with something warm and creamy, like Scotch Chicken (see page 56). And it's best to avoid mixing metaphors: an assortment of Latin-inspired hors d'oeuvres makes a far more pleasing spread than a couple of Latin dishes paired with sushi and Chinese egg rolls.

One last thought on composing your menu: Select hors d'oeuvres with an eye to logistics. If your guests will be standing and poising a glass of wine in one hand, serve finger food only. It's not hard to juggle a plateful of food and a full glass—until you want to taste the food!

About Wines and Spirits

Whether you choose to offer your guests wine, cocktails, neither, or both, one thing is clear: It's unwise to serve alcoholic beverages without a little food to cushion them. If you're controlling the bar, start off slowly. Make the first round a little less stiff than usual, and bring on some food right away. And you don't need to fill glasses the minute they're empty—bad manners, perhaps, but good sense.

What you choose to pour with hors d'oeuvres is certainly a matter of personal taste, although you'll find beverage suggestions throughout this book. Wine is almost always a good choice, and increasingly popular. In general, the best appetizer wines are light-bodied, crisp, and fruity. Among whites, the dry Alsatian Rieslings and Gewürztraminers can stand up to slightly spicy foods particularly well. Fruity California Chenin Blancs and French Chenin Blanc from the Loire Valley are lovely with fish, shellfish, and pork. The crisp California Sauvignon Blancs are excellent fish and hors d'oeuvre wines, as are many of the simple whites from Italy.

Among reds, the fruity Beaujolais wines are delightful with pâtés and grilled foods. Beaujolais is a versatile, likeable red that marries well with many dishes; if you're only pouring one wine, it's a good choice.

California Zinfandels made in a light style, simple French Côtes-du-Rhône, Spanish reds from Rioja, and light-bodied Italian Chiantis can also make good appetizer wines, and most are modestly priced.

Pickled or spicy hors d'oeuvres—for example, Texas-Style Cocktail Ribs (see page 54), Seviche (see page 42), or Pork in Green Chile (see page 58)—present problems for wine and may be better with cocktails or beer.

You'll find Champagne mentioned often as a partner to hors d'oeuvres, for it is an appetizer par excellence. Its high acid content stimulates the gastric juices; its fresh, clean flavors awake the palate, and its bubbles lighten the spirit. With pâtés, fish, and shellfish it is truly at its best. There are dozens of excellent values in sparkling wine made by the Champagne method, from California, Italy, Spain, and France. Ask your wine merchant for recommendations.

Compiling a Well-Stocked Larder

"Won't you come in for a drink?"

"Please bring your sister by for a glass of wine. We'd love to meet her."

"I couldn't get reservations until 9 p.m. Why don't we have a cocktail here first?"

Those are gracious words, and so easy to say if you keep a few supplies on hand. Your "emergency kit" need not conform to any prescribed list. Instead, it should consist of foods that fit your taste and style—items that you know you can turn into an appetizer in 15 minutes.

A few personal favorites are listed below, with some tips on what to do with them when the doorbell unexpectedly rings.

Corn Tortillas Keep them in the freezer. They thaw quickly in a slow oven and can then be cut into wedges, fried in hot oil, and sprinkled with salt.

Pita Bread Keep pita bread in the freezer. Thaw slightly in a warm oven; split the bread into two rounds and cut each round into wedges. Brush wedges with melted butter or olive oil, dust with some minced herbs or Parmesan, and bake in a moderate oven until crisp and toasty.

Anchovies Anchovies can be mashed with garlic and oil, or worked into softened butter, then spread on warm toasts.

Hard-Boiled Eggs Hard-boiled eggs are a welcome addition to any hors d'oeuvres platter. Serve them with a dollop of homemade anchovy mayonnaise or a mayonnaise heightened with mustard or capers. Or make a modest egg salad with warm chopped egg, minced parsley, and a fresh mayonnaise, then spread it lightly on toasted bread.

Olives Good olives can be served as is, or tossed with finely minced garlic and herbs and a little olive oil, or even warmed briefly in olive oil and finished with a squeeze of lemon.

Nuts Toss shelled almonds, pecans, or walnuts in melted butter, then spread on a cookie sheet and bake in a 300° F oven until fragrant. Salt to taste before serving.

Maintaining a well-stocked larder to cover spur-of-the-moment needs is a wise "entertainment insurance" policy. Drop-in guests can be accommodated easily if your pantry offers such staples as salami, olives, eggs, anchovies, and good bread or crackers.

Handsome bowls or baskets and unusual serving pieces can make an hors d'oeuvre irresistible. And don't overlook fresh flowers and herbs as colorful garnishes for trays and buffets.

Parmesan Cheese Imported Parmesan can be thinly sliced with a cheese plane and served with Toasted Bread Rounds (see page 30). Or it can be grated and dusted on oiled bread rounds before baking.

Salami Slice a first-rate dried salami paper-thin, arrange the slices in overlapping circles on a large platter, and serve with olives or radishes and a little good bread and butter.

Sun-Dried Tomatoes This new arrival on the fancy food shelves makes a splendid hors d'oeuvre when sliced in thin strips and served atop Toasted Bread Rounds (see page 30), perhaps with a paper-thin slice of Parmesan. Also available is a purée of sun-dried tomatoes, very tasty spread on warm, garlic-rubbed toast.

Good Bread Good bread for toasting should always be kept on hand in the pantry or in the freezer. It should have a good, honest flavor and a fairly dense texture. Thaw slightly if necessary, then follow directions for Toasted Bread Rounds (see page 30).

Serve It With Flair

As people in the party-giving business know, the difference between good food and great food is often presentation. The best caterers know how to "style" food, to present it in such an eye-catching way that you can't help but want some. They know how to use "props" like baskets and flowers to best effect, and they are constantly on the lookout for imaginative serving ideas. Many of the tricks of their trade are perfectly suited to home entertaining. When you need a container, for example, be creative! Do you have an empty fishbowl that you could use for a salad or candies? A copper teapot or a clear vase that you could fill with skewered foods? Tiny Japanese sake cups make clever containers for seafood. Or set out terracotta flower pots filled with an assortment of crudités. You can even use a good-looking department store box lined with tissue or bright napkins as a holder for muffins, herbed brioches, or little sandwiches.

Baskets of various shapes and sizes make handsome containers that can be used for both buffets and passed food. Fill them with Roasted Chestnuts (see page 12), Homemade Potato Chips (see page 36), or Pumpkin Satchels (see page 76). You can fill baskets with napkin-wrapped silverware or cherry tomatoes or with a "still life" of crudités (see photograph on page 35). Arrange a basket of whole seasonal vegetables into a "just-for-looks" centerpiece, or poise the basket on its side to make a cascading cornucopia of seasonal produce.

When setting up a buffet, try to include a few serving pieces or a flower arrangement that will add height to the spread. Make the hot foods most accessible, and if you consider any particular dish a show-stopper, be sure to put it front and center. If you have a choice, use an off-white or cream-colored table-cloth; most foods look better against these colors than they do against stark white linens.

Colorful food on a contrasting tray can be an appetizing sight in itself, but a less picturesque tray can be perked up with a flowery garnish—a splendid rose, orchid, or gardenia, for example. Don't get too caught up in artful arrangements, however. Guests may hesitate to help them-selves if the food looks like a careful-ly wrought still life. Oriental hors d'oeuvres such as sushi do take well to such studied presentations, but most foods look more inviting in casual settings. A heap of ribs or skewered chicken on a platter, a basket piled high with scones or Camembert Shortbread (page 21)—such "arrangements" have a look of abundance and seem to say, "Go ahead! This food is meant to be eaten!"

If you're passing food on trays, make sure it's easy to pick up. Guests shouldn't have to worry about olive oil dribbling down their shirts; save the messy, runny hors d'oeuvres for the buffet table. With food that leaves some debris behind, such as skewered foods, be sure to provide for easy disposal—perhaps a small bas-ket or glass bowl on the same tray.

To replenish a buffet gracefully, keep filled backup trays and bowls in the kitchen. Then, when the squid salad begins to look depleted, you can bring out a fresh bowl and whisk the old one away.

How Much Is Enough?

Knowing how many hors d'oeuvres to make, and how much of each one, takes common sense coupled with some educated guesswork. If your hors d'oeuvres will be followed by a full-course dinner, keep them few and simple. For dinner parties of eight or fewer, serve a single hors d'oeuvre like Deviled Mussels (page 43) or Gazpacho Pâté (page 24). As the guest list grows, add another selection or two, but that's all; two or three pre-dinner hors d'oeuvres are sufficient no matter how large the party. Count five to six "bites" per person during the standard cock-tail hour. For example, for sixteen guests, you might make two batches of Drunken Shrimp (page 46, 40 "bites") and one batch of Zucchini Fritters (page 35, 48 "bites").

If the hors d'oeuvres are replacing dinner, figure ten to twelve "bites" per guest and offer five or six choices. A party for 40 might feature:

☐ Two batches of Mushroom and Toasted Pecan Pâté (page 27, 24 to 30 "bites")

☐ Two batches of Cabbage Tourte (page 79, 80 "bites")

☐ Three batches of Scotch Chicken (page 56, 72 "bites")

☐ Three batches of Prosciutto and Red Peppers (page 36, 75 "bites")

☐ Three portions of Sake Clams (page 45, 72 "bites")

☐ Baskets of crudités with 4 cups (1 cup should serve about twelve peo-ple) of Greek Cucumber Sauce with Spinach and Dill (page 38).

Of course heartier hors d'oeuvres like Texas-Style Cocktail Ribs (page 54) or Pollo Pequeño (page 56) go farther than nuts or olives—but that's just common sense. If you're concerned about having enough, make 10 to 20 percent extra of any items you can use as leftovers: sauces or pickles that will keep for a while, or tarts and meatballs that can be frozen.

Managing Your Time

As your guest list and your hors d'oeuvre selection increase, so must your organization. No host wants to be stuck in the kitchen while the party's going on, but that means some concentrated pre-party planning and effort. In composing your menu, keep to a minimum the dishes that need last-minute at-tention. One sautéed or deep-fried dish is all you can reasonably handle without help. Round out the menu with a few dishes that can be made entirely ahead, and one or two that need only be baked, grilled, or reheated.

If you will be using tart shells or crêpes, you can make them weeks ahead and freeze them. Pickled vege-tables can be made days or weeks ahead. The day before the party, you can make most pâtés and many tart fillings, grate cheese, make bread crumbs, toast nuts, and trim or cube meats.

When you won't have much time to prepare, consider selecting from among the following quickly made dishes: Gazpacho Pâté (page 24), Pollo Pequeño (page 56), Sicil-ian Tomato Spread (page 29), Melon or Papaya with Prosciutto (page 64), Spicy Persian Lamb Balls (page 61), Baked Potato Skins (page 37), Crostini di Ricotta (page 21), Gruyère and Bacon Bites (page 18), Potted Shrimp (page 40), Garlic and Hot-Pepper Almonds (page 14), Cherry Tomatoes in Oil and Vinegar (page 110), Creole Pecans (page 12), Shrimp in Sherry Almond Butter (page 122).

In short, take the time to plan a menu that will provide the right kind of food for the occasion without overtaxing your resources. The result will be a party that you enjoy as much as your guests do.

Wonderful food starts with the best ingredients—among them, flavorful produce, fresh shellfish and eggs, good pasta, and an herb vinegar.

A Repertoire for All Seasons

The idea of the appetizer is common to cuisines all over the world. From Tallahassee to Tokyo, good cooks have a repertoire of dishes to whet the appetite and set the mood. The multinational collection that follows reflects this diversity, from Russian *blini* to Moroccan Carrots to Creole Pecans. The recipes are grouped by category: Nuts and Olives, Eggs and Cheese, Pâtés and Spreadables, Vegetables (plus dipping sauces), Fish and Shellfish, Meats and Poultry, Fruits, and Pastry- and Bread-Based Hors d'Oeuvres (including cocktail pizzas). Whether you're planning a backyard hoedown or a bridal shower, you'll find appetizers to set any scene.

NUTS AND OLIVES

Every well-stocked larder should boast a variety of nuts and olives, for they are the epitome of cocktail fare: light, slightly salty, and, in the most basic sense of the word, appetizing. When people drop in for a glass of wine or a predinner cocktail, you can put out a bowl of warm mixed nuts or open a jar of olives, squeeze on some lemon, and add a drizzle of good olive oil in less time than it takes your guests to remove their coats. If you have a little more warning, you can make any of the following hors d'oeuvres in very short order. The marinated olives (see pages 14–15) require a half-day's lead time, but they can be made far ahead and put aside for the proper moment.

ROASTED CHESTNUTS

Sidewalk chestnut vendors are a familiar winter sight in New York and the cities of Europe. They tuck the steaming hot nuggets into paper cones for shoppers and strollers, who probably appreciate the warmth as much as the rich, nutty goodness. Try roasting chestnuts at home, to go with sherry, red wine, or hot cider. Cook them in a casserole in the oven as described below, or wrap them in heavy-duty aluminum foil and roast them outdoors over coals. You can also roast them on a grate in the fireplace, or over the "open fire," using a heavy lidded skillet with a long handle or a popcorn popper; shake the pan repeatedly until the shells pop open. They become harder to peel as they cool, so serve them hot from the cooking container or in a napkin-lined basket.

> 2 dozen chestnuts
> Olive oil
> 2 tablespoons water

1. Preheat oven to 425° F. With a small, sharp knife, cut a cross in the flat side of each chestnut. Place chestnuts in a casserole with a tight-fitting lid; add a few drops of oil and swirl the dish to coat each nut lightly. Add water and cover.

2. Bake until chestnuts feel tender when squeezed and peel easily, about 25 to 30 minutes. Remove to a napkin-lined basket or serve from the casserole.

Makes 2 dozen.

CREOLE PECANS

Louisiana flavors spice up these deep-fried nuts—a hard-to-resist companion to tequila-based drinks and beer. Choose only handsome pecan halves and, if possible, taste before you buy to make sure they're fresh and moist.

> 2 tablespoons melted butter
> 1 teaspoon each *ground cumin, celery seed, and minced garlic*
> ½ to 1 teaspoon cayenne pepper
> 1 teaspoon hot curry powder (optional)
> 1 pound shelled pecans
> Corn oil for deep-frying
> Kosher salt

1. In a bowl stir together butter, cumin, celery seed, garlic, cayenne, and curry powder (if used). Add nuts and stir to coat well. Let rest at room temperature at least 1 hour or up to 12 hours.

2. In a 9-inch skillet, heat at least 2 inches of oil to 375° F. Fry nuts in hot oil until golden and fragrant. Drain on paper towels, salt lightly, and let cool 10 minutes before serving.

Makes 1 pound.

YOUR OWN "BRIDGE MIX"

Trail mix, party mix, bridge mix, cocktail mix . . . whatever the name, it's an addicting "munchie," and best when you make your own. Fill small bowls with this nutty mix and place them strategically: on the bar, on the mantel, on the piano, or wherever guests are likely to gather. This recipe yields a large batch; store any extra in an airtight container.

> 1 pound Brazil nuts, unskinned
> 1 pound almonds, unskinned
> 1 pound blanched cashews
> ½ pound pine nuts, shelled
> ¼ pound muscat raisins or seedless dark raisins
> ⅓ pound golden raisins
> ⅓ cup Marsala or sweet vermouth
> ½ pound shelled pistachio nuts
> ¼ cup shredded unsweetened coconut
> ¼ cup lightly salted sunflower seeds
> ¼ cup finely minced dried apricots
> Kosher salt
> Worcestershire sauce (optional)

1. Preheat oven to 350° F. In separate batches, toast Brazil nuts, almonds, cashews, and pine nuts on cookie sheets until lightly browned and fragrant. Set aside to cool.

2. In a medium saucepan combine dark and golden raisins with Marsala. Bring to a boil, reduce heat, and simmer gently until liquid has evaporated, about 20 to 30 minutes. Set aside to cool.

3. Combine cooled toasted nuts with raisins, pistachios, coconut, sunflower seeds, and apricots. Add salt and Worcestershire sauce (if used) to taste.

Makes about 10 cups.

Fresh, plump chestnuts are a harbinger of autumn. Roast them yourself and serve with sherry or cider.

Storebought olives personalized with fresh herbs and citrus, Orange and Fennel Olives are an appetizer par excellence and an excellent companion to cocktails.

GARLIC AND HOT-PEPPER ALMONDS

Peppery toasted almonds make a quick nibble to accompany cocktails or wine. Take a batch to the ball game; they're excellent with beer! Almonds can be made up to two weeks ahead if stored in an airtight container.

- 2 tablespoons olive oil
- 2 tablespoons butter
- 1 tablespoon minced garlic
- ½ teaspoon dried hot red pepper flakes
- 3 cups whole blanched almonds Kosher salt

In a large skillet over moderate heat, heat olive oil and butter. When butter foams, add garlic and stir until fragrant. Add pepper flakes and stir an additional 15 seconds. Add almonds and stir continuously until nuts are well coated and lightly toasted. Add salt to taste. Drain nuts on paper towels and let cool. Serve cool but not cold.
Makes 3 cups.

ORANGE AND FENNEL OLIVES

Overnight marinating infuses these olives with the flavors of tangy citrus peel, garlic, and fennel. Use only best-quality unpitted olives here: Greek Kalamata or French Niçoise olives are good choices, if available.

- 2 pounds black olives, rinsed of any brine
  Rind of 2 oranges, orange part only, cut into strips as long as possible
  Rind of 2 lemons, yellow part only, cut into strips as long as possible
  Juice of 4 lemons
- 3 to 4 tablespoons fennel seeds
- 4 large cloves garlic, peeled

Combine olives, orange rind, lemon rind, lemon juice, fennel seeds, and garlic. Pack into clean glass jars, cover, and marinate overnight at room temperature. Olives can be stored up to 6 months in the refrigerator.
Makes 2 pounds.

ZIPPING UP STOREBOUGHT OLIVES

Buy unpitted olives, either green or black, rinse off any brine under cold running water, and then marinate them to taste. With quality oils and vinegars, fresh herbs and garlic, and freshly crushed spices, you can add new life and a personal stamp to a storebought product.

French-Style Olives

> 1 pound olives, rinsed of any brine
> ¼ cup olive oil
> 2 tablespoons walnut oil
> ½ cup pickled walnuts
> ¼ cup lemon juice
> 2 garlic cloves, peeled
>   Kosher salt

In a large, clean glass jar with lid, combine olives, olive oil, walnut oil, walnuts, lemon juice, garlic, and salt to taste. Shake well. Marinate at room temperature, shaking jar occasionally, for at least 12 hours. Serve immediately, with a little of the marinade, or store up to 6 months in the marinade in the refrigerator.
Makes 1 pound.

Greek-Style Olives

> 1 pound olives, rinsed of any brine
> ¼ cup red wine vinegar
> ⅔ cup green fruity olive oil
> 4 to 5 sprigs oregano or 2 tablespoons dried
>   Kosher salt

In a large, clean glass jar with lid, combine olives, vinegar, olive oil, oregano, and salt to taste. Shake well. Marinate at room temperature, shaking jar occasionally, for at least 12 hours. Serve immediately, with a little of the marinade and the oregano sprigs for garnish, or store up to 6 months in the marinade in the refrigerator.
Makes 1 pound.

Sicilian-Style Olives

> 1 pound olives, rinsed of any brine
> 2 tablespoons balsamic vinegar (available in specialty foodmarkets)
> 2 tablespoons lemon juice
> ¼ cup olive oil
> ½ to 1 teaspoon dried hot red pepper flakes
> 2 garlic cloves, peeled
>   Kosher salt

In a large, clean glass jar with lid, combine olives, vinegar, lemon juice, olive oil, pepper flakes, garlic, and salt to taste. Shake well. Marinate at room temperature, shaking jar occasionally, for at least 12 hours. Serve immediately in a little of the marinade, or store up to 6 months in marinade in the refrigerator.
Makes 1 pound.

California-Style Olives

> 1 pound olives, rinsed of any brine
> 2 tablespoons white wine vinegar
> 2 tablespoons tarragon vinegar
> ½ cup olive oil
> 1 jar (3 to 4 oz) cocktail onions
> 2 tarragon sprigs
> 2 parsley sprigs
>   Kosher salt

In a large, clean glass jar with lid, combine olives, vinegars, olive oil, cocktail onions, tarragon sprigs, parsley sprigs, and salt. Shake well. Marinate at room temperature, shaking jar occasionally, for at least 12 hours. Serve immediately, with a little of the marinade and the onions, and the parsley sprigs for garnish, or store up to 6 months in the marinade in the refrigerator.
Makes 1 pound.

A PARTY DRINK GUIDE

Many popular cocktails and mixed drinks are now available in packaged form. There's much to be said for their convenience, but they can't compare with the flavor of a freshly mixed drink. Whether you're entertaining hundreds or just having a few friends in for cocktails, one way to make guests feel special is to offer a mixed drink of your own creation.

PLANTER'S PUNCH

Whether this tastes as good at home as it does on a sunny tropical isle is debatable; what's clear is that it's fun and refreshing, the perfect poolside drink, and an excellent antidote to "dog days" in *any* setting.

> ¾ cup Sugar Syrup
> 1 cup fresh lime juice
> 3 cups unsweetened pineapple juice
> ½ cup light rum
> ½ cup dark rum

Sugar Syrup

> 1 cup sugar
> 2 cups water

In a shaker jar combine ¾ cup Sugar Syrup, lime and pineapple juices, and light and dark rum. Shake well, then divide mixture among 8 highball (8-oz) glasses half-filled with crushed ice.
Makes 8 drinks.

Sugar Syrup Combine sugar and water in a saucepan. Bring to a boil, stirring, over moderately high heat, then cook without stirring for 5 minutes. Cool completely. Sugar Syrup may be made ahead and stored in a glass jar in the refrigerator indefinitely.
Makes 2 cups.

EGGNOG

Yes, it's powerfully rich *and* irresist-ible—two reasons why most people permit themselves some only once a year. But is a holiday party a holiday party without a creamy, high-spirited eggnog?

- 1 dozen eggs, separated
- 2 cups superfine sugar
- 2 cups brandy
- 2 cups dark rum
- 1 cup bourbon
- 1 cup vodka
- 4 pints whipping cream
  Freshly grated nutmeg

1. In large bowl of electric mixer, beat egg yolks until light and thick, or whisk by hand. Add sugar slowly and beat until very light and fluffy. Gradually add brandy, beating well. Let mixture steep at room tem-perature for 2 hours.

2. Add rum, bourbon, and vodka to egg yolk mixture, beating well, either by hand or with electric mixer. Beat in cream. Chill mixture several hours or overnight.

3. In large mixing bowl, beat egg whites to soft peaks. Fold gently into cream mixture. Taste; adjust sugar, liquor, or cream as necessary. Serve in old-fashioned (6-oz) glasses with a dusting of nutmeg on top.
Makes a generous gallon, about twenty-four 6-ounce servings.

TEA PUNCH

There's a little more to it than tea, but the flavor of a good strong brew really does come through. Serve this colorful, fruit-filled punch at in-formal receptions or afternoon teas; it's especially suitable for outdoor entertaining—by the pool, on the boat, or in your own backyard.

- 1 cup Sugar Syrup (see page 15)
- 1 cup Cognac or brandy
- 1 cup lemon juice
- 2 cups strong tea
- 1 quart club soda
- 1 quart grapefruit soda, lemon-lime soda, or tonic water
- ½ cup sweet vermouth
- ½ cup vodka
- 3 cups seasonal fruits (peaches, pears, grapes, apples, oranges, berries), peeled if necessary and chopped coarsely

Stir together Sugar Syrup, Cognac, lemon juice, tea, club soda, grapefruit soda, vermouth, vodka, and fruit. Let steep 2 hours. Pour over a block of ice in a small punchbowl, or divide among 24 collins (12-oz) glasses half-filled with crushed ice.
Makes about 1½ gallons, about twenty-four 12-ounce servings.

BLOODY MARY MIX

Your own homemade mix will inev-itably be more fresh and lively than the storebought variety. The mix alone, poured over ice, is a tasty pick-me-up, known to most bartenders as a Virgin Mary.

- 1 tablespoon lemon juice
- ½ teaspoon celery powder
- 1 tablespoon Worcestershire sauce
- 2 drops hot-pepper sauce, or more to taste
- 2 cups tomato juice
  Salt

Combine lemon juice, celery powder, Worcestershire sauce, and hot-pepper sauce. Let steep 5 minutes. Add tomato juice and salt to taste; stir well. Taste; adjust seasoning as necessary.
Makes enough for six 7-ounce drinks.

Bloody Mary In a shaker jar com-bine 3 ounces Bloody Mary Mix and 1½ ounces vodka. Shake well; pour over ice cubes in a highball glass. Garnish with a celery stalk.

SANGRÍA

A thirst-quenching wine punch some-times has more appeal than wine or cocktails. This Spanish Sangría should have plenty of takers at warm-weather brunches and afternoon par-ties. Sliced lemons and oranges add fresh, fruity flavor, while brandy and Triple Sec give it some spunk.

- ⅓ to ½ cup sugar
- ½ cup brandy
- 5 oranges, each cut into 12 thin wedges
- 3 lemons, sliced thin
- ½ cup Triple Sec
- 10 cups dry red wine
- 1 quart club soda

1. Combine ⅓ cup sugar, the brandy, 3 of the oranges, and the lemon slices in a large bowl. Let steep 2 hours at room temperature.

2. Add Triple Sec and wine and taste, adding more sugar if desired. Add club soda, stir, and taste again. Add remaining orange wedges. Stir brisk-ly. Pour over a block of ice in a punchbowl, or divide among glasses half-filled with cracked ice.
Makes 1 gallon, about 20 servings.

KIR

The French black-currant liqueur called *crème de cassis* is a specialty of the Dijon region. The following aperitif, created to showcase cassis, is named after its inventor, Monsieur Kir, a former mayor of Dijon. If you substitute Champagne for the white wine, it's a Kir Royale, as pretty as it is delicious.

- 1 tablespoon crème de cassis
- 6 ounces dry white wine, preferably a French Mâcon

Pour crème de cassis in the bottom of a chilled wine glass. Add wine, but do not stir. Cassis will spread itself through the wine as the glass is swirled.
Makes 1 drink.

HOW TO STOCK A HOME BAR

"Be prepared" is as good a motto for the home bartender as it is for the Boy Scouts. Here's a practical guide to the home bar, with suggested equipment and supplies, some purchasing and pouring guidelines, and some mixing dos and don'ts.

Spirits

Dry vermouth
Sweet vermouth
Dry sherry
Medium sherry
Vodka
Gin
Tequila
Puerto Rican rum
Jamaican rum
Bourbon whiskey
Scotch whiskey
Canadian whiskey
Blended whiskey
Rye
Brandy or Cognac
Benedictine
Crème de menthe
Crème de cacao
Kahlua
Triple Sec
Grand Marnier
Pernod
Cream liqueurs

Equipment

Cocktail shaker
Electric blender
Muddler
Ice bucket
Flat cocktail strainer
Jigger
Corkscrew
Combination bottle cap remover/can opener
Lemon peeler
Bar spoons (or iced-tea spoons)
Stainless steel paring knife
Lemon juicer
Swizzle sticks
Cocktail napkins
Towels
Cutting board
Ice tongs

Supplies

Ice
Bitters
Sugar Syrup (see page 15)
Carbonated water (club soda)
Tonic water
Bitter lemon
Ginger ale
Cola
Lemons
Limes
Oranges
Maraschino cherries
Cocktail onions
Green olives (pitted, unstuffed)
Sugar, superfine and powdered
Grenadine
Tomato juice
Pineapple juice
Grapefruit juice
Eggs

Some Rules of Thumb

1. Pour one 1½-ounce shot (a jigger) per drink. A 750-milliliter bottle will yield 15 to 16 drinks at 1½ ounces. For mixed drinks, use 1½ shots (jiggers) to 3 ounces of mixer.

2. Figure three drinks per person per 2 hours.

3. To determine quantities of mixers to have on hand, figure on half the drinks being served straight and half mixed.

Mixing Dos and Don'ts

1. Always make one round at a time. Discard any "overpour," which would dilute the following round.

2. Always use the best ingredients—the best liquors, the best juices, the best mixers. A bad mixer can spoil even the best liquor.

3. Never reuse the ice in your shaker.

4. Shake vigorously those cocktails meant to be shaken; don't "rock."

5. Measure ingredients carefully.

6. Use fresh lemons, limes, and oranges for juice.

7. Use superfine or powdered sugar where sugar is called for; it dissolves more easily.

8. Don't serve overly sweet or overly creamy drinks before dinner.

9. Use cracked ice or ice cubes for shaken drinks; shaved ice melts too fast and dilutes the drink before it chills it.

10. Make sure carbonated beverages are fresh and cold. Do not use if flat. Always add carbonated beverages and mixers last.

EGGS AND CHEESE

The deviled egg and the cheese ball will always be with us (thank goodness!), but the incredible egg and the many cheeses now available offer much more. Indeed, you should consider them the starting point for endless experimentation. Instead of Gruyère in Monsieur Tartine (at right), try a hot-pepper Jack. Toasted Bread Rounds with Walnuts and Blue Cheese (see page 21) would be wonderful—maybe better!—with goat cheese instead.

But as you follow these recipes, or as you deviate from them, there's one important point to remember: You get what you pay for. Good cheese is not inexpensive, but buying less-than-first-quality cheese is a false economy. Many of the packaged supermarket cheeses have had the flavor all but leached out of them. It's best to develop a good relationship with a reputable cheese merchant who will let you touch, smell, and taste to find what you like.

STILTON CROCK WITH PORT WINE

The wedge of blue-veined Stilton cheese and decanter of port are a venerable British tradition, usually served in "the drawing room" at the end of a formal meal. But this made-for-each-other pair can also be packed into a handsome crock for a pre-dinner spread, the flavors melding during the course of a week-long aging. If you are hosting a large party, you can order a whole wheel of Stilton (usually in 10- or 16-pound pieces). Slice off the top and scoop out the cheese, leaving a sturdy wall all around. Then mash the cheese with about one bottle of port, refill the wheel, and replace the cover for aging. It makes an impressive buffet centerpiece, especially at holiday time. Serve with cocktails or a hearty red wine.

  2 *pounds English Stilton cheese*
  ⅓ *to ½ cup imported port wine*
    Toasted Bread Rounds (see page 30)

1. Trim any rind from cheese; place cheese in a bowl. Add port. With back of a wooden spoon, meld port and cheese. Pack into a 4-cup crock, cover with plastic wrap, refrigerate, and let age 1 week.

2. Bring cheese to room temperature and serve with warm Toasted Bread Rounds.
Makes 4 cups, or enough for 20 to 30 cocktail servings.

MONSIEUR TARTINE

All over France, in small cafes and quick lunch spots, you'll find Croque-Monsieur on the menu. Roughly speaking, it's a grilled ham-and-cheese sandwich—golden-crusted outside and molten within. When made open-face, it becomes a tartine and a delectable cocktail nibble. Chopped tomato turns up in only a few versions, but it adds a lively color and flavor.

  ½ *pound Gruyère cheese, grated*
  2 *tablespoons flour*
  1 *teaspoon salt*
  2 *eggs, lightly beaten*
  1 *tablespoon brandy*
  ¼ *pound sliced bacon, cooked and crumbled, or ¼ pound ham, minced*
  ½ *cup peeled, seeded, and chopped tomatoes*
  2 *tablespoons finely minced red onion*
    Freshly ground black pepper to taste
  24 *two-inch bread rounds, cut with a cookie cutter*
  2 *tablespoons freshly grated Parmesan cheese*

1. Preheat oven to 450° F or preheat broiler (to medium, if possible). In a large bowl combine Gruyère, flour, salt, eggs, brandy, bacon, tomatoes, onion, and black pepper; mixture should be highly seasoned.

2. Divide mixture among bread rounds; dust with Parmesan. Bake for 6 to 7 minutes, or broil, watching closely, for 3 to 4 minutes. Serve immediately.
Makes 2 dozen cocktail-sized tartines.

Make-Ahead Tip The cheese topping can be mixed up to 6 hours ahead and assembled on bread rounds. Bake just before serving.

GRUYÈRE AND BACON BITES

Gruyère, good bacon, and thick sour cream figure in many a traditional Alsatian dish. Here they are bound with egg, heightened with pepper, and broiled on Toasted Bread Rounds. The result is a warm, smoky mouthful to serve with a dry Alsatian Riesling.

  ¼ *pound Gruyère cheese, grated*
  1 *egg, lightly beaten*
  ¼ *cup sour cream*
  ¼ *cup ricotta*
    Salt, freshly ground black pepper, and cayenne pepper to taste
  24 *Toasted Bread Rounds (see page 30)*
  ¼ *pound thick-sliced hickory-smoked bacon*

1. Preheat broiler. In a small bowl combine Gruyère, egg, sour cream, and ricotta. Add salt, black pepper, and cayenne to taste. Divide mixture among Toasted Bread Rounds.

2. Cut bacon slices into 1-inch lengths. Top each bread round with a piece of bacon. Broil rounds until bacon is crisp and browned and cheese is bubbly (about 3 minutes). Serve immediately.
Makes 2 dozen "bites."

Make-Ahead Tip Bread rounds can be topped with cheese mixture and bacon up to 6 hours ahead. Broil just before serving.

A crock of English Stilton cheese mixed with mellow port makes a royal spread for small toasts or crackers.

Sharp American Cheddar enlivens these creamy two-bite tartlets. Deceptively dainty, undeniably rich, they make marvelous finger fare for stand-up cocktail parties.

3. Divide cheese cubes among tartlet shells and top with cream mixture. Bake tartlets until well browned (12 to 15 minutes). Cool slightly, then garnish with chopped chives and serve.

Makes 2 dozen tartlets.

AMERICAN CHEDDAR TARTLETS

Eggs, cream, and sharp American Cheddar cheese bake to golden richness in these tiny cocktail tarts. Garnish with a sprinkling of chopped chives and serve with Beaujolais or a light California red wine.

> Pâte Brisée (see page 72), chilled
> ½ pound sharp American Cheddar cheese
> 4 eggs, lightly beaten
> 1 cup each whipping cream and half-and-half
> Salt, freshly ground black pepper, nutmeg, and cayenne pepper to taste
> ¼ cup chopped chives

1. Preheat oven to 350° F. Use Pâte Brisée to line 24 two-inch tartlet tins. Chill 30 minutes.

2. Cut cheese into ⅛-inch cubes. In a small bowl combine eggs, whipping cream, half-and-half, and salt, black pepper, nutmeg, and cayenne to taste.

HOMEMADE BOURSIN

The deliciously soft, spreadable French cheese called Boursin most often turns up in the American market flavored with herbs and garlic. It's a great idea in theory, but in fact, the herbs and garlic don't have much "shelf life." For a truly fresh and fragrant Boursin, try making your own.

Homemade Boursin is a matter of minutes and is one of the most versatile items you can have in your repertoire. In place of the parsley and chives specified in the recipe below, you can substitute thyme, dill, cilantro, chervil, oregano, mint, basil, anchovies, or crushed dried hot pepper flakes. Spread the cheese on warm Crêpes (see page 22), Cocktail Crumpets (see page 79), or Toasted Bread Rounds (see page 30). Stuff it into mushroom caps, endive leaves, or snow peas. The mixture can be made a week ahead, but it is at its best on the second day.

> 1 pound cream cheese
> 1 cup sour cream
> ¼ cup whole-milk yogurt
> ¼ cup unsalted butter, room temperature
> 1 tablespoon each minced garlic, minced chives, and minced parsley
> Salt, freshly ground black pepper, and cayenne pepper to taste

Combine all ingredients in a food processor or blender and blend until mixture is very smooth. Pack into a serving bowl or crock and refrigerate, covered with plastic wrap, for up to 1 week. Serve at room temperature.

Makes about 2 pounds.

QUESO FLAMEADO

"Flamed cheese" is a specialty of Guadalajara and popular in the Mexican restaurants of Texas. It could not be more artless—or more irresistible: a pool of mild melted cheese laced with spicy Mexican sausage, presented on a hot platter with a basket of tortillas or freshly fried chips. You scoop up the spicy mixture while it's hot and runny, and down it with a cold Mexican beer or a shot of tequila.

>   1   pound mozzarella cheese, grated
>   1   pound jack cheese, grated
> 1½   pounds chorizo (spicy Mexican sausage)
>   Fresh tortilla chips, homemade or storebought

1. Preheat oven to 250° F. Put an ovenproof serving platter in the oven to heat through. Combine cheeses in top of double boiler, set over simmering water, and let cheeses melt slowly.

2. In a small skillet over moderate heat, sauté sausage until cooked through. Drain off and discard fat. Add sausage to melting cheese. When cheese is fully melted and very hot, pour onto hot serving platter. Serve with a basket of tortilla chips.

Makes enough for 15 generous portions.

CROSTINI DI RICOTTA

"Little crusts" of French or Italian bread are topped with a fennel-laced mixture of sausage and cheese, then broiled until bubbly—a sort of mini-pizza, quickly made. The topping also makes a marvelous open-faced sandwich mounded on thick bread slices.

> 1½   pounds ricotta cheese
>   ½   cup freshly grated Parmesan cheese
>   ¼   cup grated Romano cheese
>   3   tablespoons olive oil
>   3   cloves garlic, minced
>   3 to 4 hot Italian sausages, about 4 inches long

> 1½   tablespoons fennel seed
>   Salt and freshly ground black pepper to taste
>   36   two-and-a-half-inch oblong slices or rounds of French bread

1. Preheat broiler. In a large bowl combine ricotta, Parmesan, and Romano cheeses. In a heavy skillet over moderate heat, heat olive oil. Add garlic and cook 45 seconds. Add sausages and cook slowly until they are well browned and cooked through (15 to 20 minutes). Remove from pan and cool completely, then remove casings.

2. Crumble sausage and add to cheeses, along with any oil and garlic in the sauté pan. Add fennel seed, and salt and pepper to taste; mix well.

3. Spread cheese mixture on bread slices and broil until bubbly and lightly browned. Serve immediately.

Makes 3 dozen crostini.

TOASTED BREAD ROUNDS WITH WALNUTS AND BLUE CHEESE

A smooth walnut paste is spread on basil-scented bread rounds, then topped with crumbled Gorgonzola cheese. Served hot and bubbly, the toasted rounds make a robust companion to Chianti or Zinfandel.

>   24   Toasted Bread Rounds, with 2 tablespoons minced fresh basil or 2 teaspoons dried basil added to oil mixture (see page 30)
>   ¼   pound walnuts, finely ground
>   1   teaspoon minced garlic
>   1   teaspoon walnut oil (see Note)
>   ⅓   pound Gorgonzola or other strong blue cheese, crumbled
>   Additional fresh basil, cut in thin strips (optional)

Preheat oven to 350° F. Place ground walnuts, garlic, and walnut oil in blender or food processor and blend to make a smooth paste. Spread 2 teaspoons of this mixture on each of the bread rounds, top each round

with some of the crumbled cheese, and bake until cheese is bubbly. If desired, garnish with additional fresh basil; serve immediately.

Makes 2 dozen cocktail bread rounds.

Make-Ahead Tip Ground walnut mixture can be made up to 1 month ahead. Store in a covered jar in the refrigerator.

Note If necessary, olive oil may be substituted for the walnut oil.

CAMEMBERT SHORTBREAD

Here's a savory variation on a classic, with all the rich crumbly goodness that traditional shortbread is known for. For best results, have all ingredients very cold. Cool the shortbread to room temperature before serving—with red wine and Garlic and Hot-Pepper Almonds (see page 14) before dinner, or after dinner with a glass of port. You can store the shortbread in an airtight tin for up to 2 weeks.

>   2   cups sifted flour
>   1   teaspoon salt
>   ¼   cup unsalted butter, chilled
>   3   ounces ripe Camembert cheese, chilled
>   3   eggs, lightly beaten

1. Preheat oven to 400° F. Combine flour and salt in a food processor fitted with steel blade. Process briefly to combine. Add butter, cheese, and eggs, and process just until a soft dough forms; don't overwork it. To form dough by hand, stir together flour and salt. Cut in butter and cheese until mixture is crumbly. Add eggs; stir just to combine.

2. With floured hands, gently pat dough into a 10-inch circle. Place circle on a well-buttered baking sheet; cut into 16 wedges. Bake until lightly browned all over (20 to 25 minutes). Cool on a rack before serving.

Makes 16 wedges.

COLD OMELET ROLLS WITH AVOCADO AND SMOKED SALMON

Like Japanese sushi, these chilled omelet rolls are visually striking—a spiral of yellow, pink, and green that tastes as good as it looks. Arranged on a black lacquered tray, they are simply stunning, the perfect partner to a glass of Champagne or icy vodka.

- 6 eggs
  Salt
- 2 tablespoons butter
- 1 large or 2 small avocados
- 1½ tablespoons lemon juice
- 3 ounces smoked salmon, in small pieces

1. In a small bowl break 1 egg and beat lightly. Add a pinch of salt. In a 6-inch skillet over moderately high heat, melt 1 teaspoon of the butter. Add egg mixture and swirl to coat pan. Cook until egg is just set, then slide out onto a plate. Repeat with remaining eggs and butter to make six flat omelets.

2. In a small bowl mash avocado well; add lemon juice and salt to taste. Lay cooled omelets out flat on a work surface; arrange morsels of smoked salmon in a line down the center of each. Spread some of the avocado mixture over the omelets, to within ¼ inch of the edges. Roll the omelets into cylinders and chill.

3. To serve, cut each cylinder on the diagonal into four oblong slices. Arrange slices on a platter and serve chilled.

Makes 2 dozen bite-sized omelet rolls.

PICKLED EGGS

Walk into almost any English pub and you'll spot a jar of pickled eggs on the bar. Patrons down them with pints of ale for a quick and nourishing snack, or add cheese and a chunk of bread and call it lunch. As hors d'oeuvres, they can be served sliced atop buttered dark bread, or halved as a garnish for a platter of cold meats. They are exceptionally easy to make, and they keep well; store them in a covered glass jar in the refrigerator for up to 1 month. If you can find them, pickle tiny quail eggs for a particularly whimsical addition to the buffet table.

- 1 dozen eggs
- 3 cups cider vinegar
- 3 cups water
- 2 tablespoons mixed pickling spice
- 1 medium onion, sliced
- 1 teaspoon salt

1. Put eggs in a large pot, cover with cold water, and bring to a boil. Boil gently for 6 minutes, then drain and chill under running cold water. Peel eggs.

2. In a saucepan combine vinegar, water, pickling spice, onion, and salt. Bring just to a boil, then remove from heat and let cool 15 minutes. Pack eggs into a large, clean glass jar and pour in warm liquid; let cool, then cover and refrigerate at least 1 day before using.

Makes 1 dozen eggs.

CRÊPES COLD AND HOT

Basic Crêpe Batter

Make this recipe in a large bowl, then transfer half at a time to the blender for a final smoothing. Feel free to flavor the batter to complement your filling: with chopped fresh dill, parsley, chervil, lemon peel, garlic, green onions . . .

- 6 eggs
- ⅔ cup half-and-half
- 1 cup water
- 1¼ cups milk
- 2 cups flour
- 2 tablespoons butter, melted
- 1 tablespoon sugar
- 1 teaspoon salt
- ¼ cup brandy or Cognac
  Additional butter for cooking crêpes

1. In a large bowl combine eggs, half-and-half, water, milk, flour, the melted butter, sugar, salt, and brandy and whisk together well. Batter will be slightly lumpy. Transfer batter to blender in batches and blend until smooth. Let batter rest at room temperature 45 minutes or refrigerate overnight before using.

2. Heat a nonstick 7-inch skillet or crêpe pan over moderately high heat. Add a teaspoon of butter and swirl to coat the pan. When butter foams, add 3 tablespoons batter and quickly tilt pan to coat bottom of skillet evenly. Cook crêpe just until set, about 45 to 60 seconds, then use a spatula to transfer it to a sheet of waxed paper. Continue with remaining batter. Do not stack crêpes until they are all completely cool.

Makes about 3 dozen crêpes.

Make-Ahead Tip Completely cooled crêpes may be stacked, wrapped in foil, and refrigerated for up to 5 days or frozen for up to 2 months.

Crêpes Cold

Use cooled (but not chilled) crêpes in any of the following ways:

□ Wrapped around pencil-thin asparagus.

□ Spread with chutney, then topped with paper-thin smoked ham or turkey and rolled up like a cigarette.

□ Halved and spread with any of the following fillings, then folded into a triangle or rolled up cornucopia style:

1. Goat cheese and Tapenade (see page 29)

2. Smoked salmon and avocado

3. Prosciutto and Red Peppers (see page 36)

4. Paper-thin slices of Gruyère and ham, with a swipe of Dijon mustard

5. Ricotta and sliced sun-dried tomatoes mixed with chopped parsley or chives and minced garlic.

Crêpes Hot

Wrap hot-off-the-griddle crêpes around the following fillings:

□ Curried Crab (see page 42)

□ Tiny shrimp warmed in a saucepan with a little sour cream, chopped tomatoes, shallots, and thyme

□ Sausage and cheese (use topping for Crostini di Ricotta, page 21)

□ Crumbled blue cheese and chopped walnuts

□ Grated Gruyère and crumbled bacon

Crêpazes

A "short stack" of crêpes, with a savory filling between the layers, can be warmed through in the oven, then cut into wedges.

    8 *Basic Crêpes (see page 22), plain or herbed*

    ¼ *pound Westphalian ham or boiled ham, sliced thin*

    ¼ *pound Emmentaler or similar imported Swiss cheese, sliced thin*

    3 *tablespoons butter*

    2 *tablespoons freshly grated Parmesan cheese*

    2 *tablespoons sour cream*

    2 *tablespoons chopped chives*

1. Preheat oven to 375° F. On a buttered cookie sheet, stack two crêpes. Top them with slices of ham and cheese and dot with butter. Repeat until all crêpes are used up.

2. Dust top with Parmesan. Bake until crêpes are lightly browned and edges are slightly crispy (10 to 15 minutes). Let cool slightly, then cut into wedges. Serve immediately, with a dab of sour cream and a sprinkling of chives.

Makes about 10 wedges.

HOW TO MAKE CRÊPES

The secret to making good crêpes is to maintain a steady medium-hot temperature.

1. *Pour batter into greased pan, tilting pan so batter forms a thin, even covering over entire bottom.*

2. *Cook crêpe 45 to 60 seconds. Small holes will be visible on top side; bottom will be browned.*

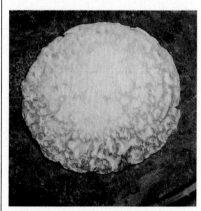

3. *Remove crêpe to a platter, board, or sheet of waxed paper to cool (do not turn to cook second side).*

PÂTÉS AND SPREADABLES

A little something smooth and creamy on a cracker or toast is one of the most popular kinds of hors d'oeuvres—and, since the advent of the food processor, one of the easiest. Foods that otherwise might be messy or require a knife and fork can be blended, seasoned, bound with butter, cream, or cheese, and packed into a crock or a handsome mold. Of course, good bread, crackers, or bread rounds to hold up these "spreadables" is an essential part of the equation.

For small, informal gatherings, set a pâté on the cocktail table with toasts in a basket alongside and let guests help themselves. For larger stand-up parties, you'll need to spend a little time in the kitchen composing canapés that can be arranged on trays to be circulated among your guests. Spreadables are a little awkward at a cocktail buffet, but that's the perfect occasion for a homemade pâté or terrine, sliced and arranged on a platter with an appropriate mustard or mayonnaise.

The advantage of *all* the following pâtés and spreadables is that they can—and in many cases should—be made in advance. There's no last-minute preparation to leave you greasy and flustered or to keep you away from the conversation. What's more, all of the recipes that follow are readily portable—to potlucks, picnics, and office parties, or to another dinner party as a housegift for the host.

The classic pâté, by definition, is always encased in a pastry crust. The classic terrine, on the other hand, is a sort of pâté-without-a-crust, named for the earthenware dish it is baked in. Few people except the French make those distinctions any longer; most American restaurants and cookbooks use the words interchangeably. In fact, you'll find several "pâtés" in this chapter, but not one in a pastry crust!

GAZPACHO PÂTÉ

Nothing speaks more of summer than the flavors of gazpacho. This molded version makes a refreshing hot-weather first course or a striking addition to a summer buffet. Spread on Hallie's Corn Crackers (see page 30), melba toast, or leaves of Belgian endive.

> 2 pounds plum tomatoes, chopped, with their juice, or 1 can (about 2 lbs) plum tomatoes with their juice
> 1 cucumber, peeled, seeded, and chopped
> 1 green pepper, seeded, deribbed, and chopped
> 1 onion, chopped
> 3 tablespoons olive oil
> 2 tablespoons red wine vinegar
> 2 tablespoons tomato paste
> 2½ teaspoons salt
> 1½ teaspoons ground cumin
> ½ teaspoon each celery seed and cayenne pepper
> 3 tablespoons (3 envelopes) unflavored gelatin
> ½ cup white wine
> 2 large avocados, peeled and cubed
> 1 cup minced green pepper

1. Purée tomatoes, cucumber, green pepper, onion, olive oil, vinegar, tomato paste, salt, cumin, celery seed, and cayenne in a food processor or in batches in a blender.

2. Sprinkle gelatin over wine in a small bowl, then set bowl in a pan of hot water and stir until gelatin is dissolved. Add to purée along with avocados and minced green pepper.

3. Pour mixture into an oiled 6-cup loaf pan. Chill thoroughly before serving.
Makes about 25 servings.

QUICK COUNTRY PÂTÉ

A coarse, "peasant-style" beef and pork combination that's great for picnics or informal parties, this pâté doesn't even require a loaf pan. Set it out with tiny French *cornichons* (pickles), a crock of Dijon mustard, sliced baguettes, and a bottle of Beaujolais. Cold and thinly sliced on French bread, it makes a splendid next-day sandwich.

> 1 pound lean ground pork
> 1½ pounds lean ground beef
> 1 large onion, minced
> 3 large cloves garlic, minced
> ¼ cup minced green onion
> ½ cup fresh bread crumbs
> 3 eggs, lightly beaten
> 1 teaspoon minced fresh thyme or ½ teaspoon dried
> ½ teaspoon ground bay leaves
> 1½ teaspoons black pepper
> Salt
> ½ pound thickly sliced hickory-smoked bacon

1. Preheat oven to 325° F. In a large bowl combine all ingredients except bacon. Work mixture together thoroughly but lightly, preferably with your hands. Fry a little bit of the mixture and taste; adjust seasonings if necessary.

2. Lay the bacon slices out on a baking sheet, side by side and barely touching. Form the meat into a loaf shape and place it across the middle of the bacon slices. Bring ends of bacon up around the loaf to enclose it. Turn loaf over so that ends of bacon are underneath.

3. Bake the loaf until well browned and very firm (1½ hours). Baste frequently with any fat that drains from the meat. Cool completely before slicing.
Serves 16 to 20.

Hickory-smoked bacon flavors and moistens Quick Country Pâté, a casual first course to serve with pungent mustard and pickles.

Serve creamy Layered Crab and Spinach Terrine as a cocktail spread or let it launch an elegant dinner party. Spinach combined with cream sauce makes up the center, with a sour-cream-and-crab mixture for the top and bottom layers.

LAYERED CRAB AND SPINACH TERRINE

Alternate layers of white and green make for a visually striking production. Use it as part of a winter buffet or serve as the first course in a sit-down dinner with a dill mayonnaise and a California Chardonnay.

Crab Layer

½ pound fresh crabmeat, picked over and flaked
¼ cup sour cream
1 teaspoon lemon juice
½ teaspoon Dijon mustard
    Salt and black pepper to taste
½ teaspoon cayenne pepper
2 large eggs, lightly beaten

Spinach Layer

2 tablespoons unsalted butter
2 teaspoons flour
½ cup whipping cream
⅔ cup half-and-half
1¼ pounds cooked spinach, drained and squeezed to remove excess moisture
3 eggs
½ teaspoon black pepper
¼ teaspoon ground nutmeg
½ teaspoon sugar
    Salt to taste

1. Preheat oven to 375° F. *For the crab layer:* In a medium bowl combine the crab, sour cream, lemon juice, mustard, salt, pepper, and cayenne. Stir in eggs and set mixture aside.

2. *For the spinach layer:* Melt butter in a heavy saucepan until foamy. Whisk in flour and cook for 3 minutes over medium heat, stirring constantly.

3. Whisk in whipping cream and half-and-half. Bring to a boil, then reduce heat and simmer slowly 10 minutes. Stir occasionally, scraping down the sides and around the bottom as necessary. Mixture will thicken as it cooks.

4. Remove from heat and stir in spinach. Let cool. Stir in eggs, one at a time, then add black pepper, nutmeg, sugar, and salt.

5. *To assemble the terrine:* Grease an 8-cup loaf pan with butter. Spoon half the crab mixture into the mold and cover with all of the spinach mixture. Spoon remaining crab mixture over the spinach.

6. Set the terrine in a baking pan and pour 1 inch of hot water into the baking pan. Bake, uncovered, until golden brown and puffy (30 to 45 minutes). Cool on a rack. To serve, run a knife around the edge and invert onto a serving platter. Serve at room temperature or chilled with mayonnaise.

Serves 8.

MUSHROOM AND TOASTED-PECAN PÂTÉ

This nutty mushroom preparation is the perfect companion to a glass of dry sherry and a basket of whole wheat melba toast or dark party rye. The food processor makes an easy job of it.

- *1 pound mushrooms, cleaned and chopped*
- *¼ cup celery*
- *1 cup toasted pecans*
- *½ cup each ricotta cheese, grated Parmesan cheese, minced parsley, and minced shallots*
- *¼ cup unsalted butter*
- *1 cup freshly toasted bread crumbs*
- *2 tablespoons chopped fresh basil or 1 teaspoon dried*
- *3 sprigs fresh oregano, chopped, or ½ teaspoon dried*
- *1 teaspoon salt Cayenne and black pepper to taste*

1. Preheat oven to 400° F. In a food processor, combine mushrooms, celery, pecans, ricotta and Parmesan cheeses, and parsley. With on/off pulsing, process to mix. Mixture should be coarse.

2. In a skillet over medium heat, melt 2 tablespoons of the butter; add shallots and sauté until translucent. Add mushroom mixture, the remaining 2 tablespoons butter, bread crumbs, basil, oregano, salt, cayenne, and black pepper. Taste and adjust salt if necessary.

3. Butter an 8-cup loaf pan; line with buttered parchment paper or waxed paper. Pack pâté mixture into mold; cover top with additional buttered paper. Bake until tester inserted in center comes out clean (1 to 1½ hours). Allow to cool completely; invert onto platter just before serving. Pâté is best served cool but not cold.

Serves 12 to 15.

SMOKED FISH MOUSSE

Smoked fish and vodka go together like chocolate chip cookies and milk. Serve the vodka ice-cold and spread this luxurious mousse on warm toast, Hallie's Corn Crackers (see page 30), Walnut Scones (see page 30), or Toasted Bread Rounds made with rye or pumpernickel (see page 30). You can make this two to three days ahead.

- *3 tablespoons unsalted butter*
- *¼ cup minced shallots*
- *1 pound good-quality smoked sturgeon or whitefish, boned and flaked*
- *½ cup each sour cream and cream cheese*
- *½ cup unsalted butter, softened*
- *3 tablespoons lemon juice*
- *2 tablespoons vodka*
- *½ cup whipping cream, whipped to soft peaks Salt and cayenne pepper to taste*

1. Heat the 3 tablespoons butter in a small skillet until foamy. Sauté shallots over medium heat until soft but not browned. Add fish and mix well. Remove from heat.

2. Place mixture in food processor or blender along with sour cream, cream cheese, and the ½ cup butter. Process or blend until smooth. Add lemon juice and vodka and blend again. Remove to a bowl.

3. Fold the whipped cream into the fish mixture by hand, then add salt and cayenne. Pack into one 2½-cup mold or five ½-cup molds.

Makes 2½ cups.

DUCK LIVER PÂTÉ

This rich pâté makes an elegant start to a formal dinner, accompanied by Champagne or sparkling wine and warm toasted brioche.

- *¾ pound fresh duck livers*
- *1 cup milk*
- *3 tablespoons Armagnac or other brandy*
- *3 tablespoons unsalted butter*
- *¼ cup minced shallots*
- *1 pippin apple, peeled, cored, and coarsely chopped*
- *1 clove garlic, minced*
- *½ teaspoon cayenne pepper Salt and black pepper to taste*
- *1½ cups unsalted butter, softened*

1. Soak livers in milk for 2 hours. Drain. Cut away any membranes, then marinate livers in brandy for 1 hour. Drain; reserve brandy.

2. Heat the 3 tablespoons butter in a large skillet until bubbly; add shallots and sauté on medium heat until soft but not browned. Add apple, garlic, and livers. Sauté only until livers lose their raw color; the inside should remain slightly pink. Add cayenne, salt, and black pepper and remove from heat.

3. Purée mixture in a food processor, or in batches in a blender, along with 2 tablespoons of the brandy and the 1½ cups softened butter. Strain through a sieve. Taste; adjust salt, pepper, and brandy as necessary.

4. Pack mixture into several small molds or one 8-cup mold. Chill well.

Makes 8 cups.

*Sicilian Tomato Spread,
Mediterranean Eggplant Spread,
and Tapenade make
mouthwatering toppings and dips
for breads and crackers.*

TAPENADE

An earthy olive spread from southern France, *tapenade* (pronounced TOP-eh-nod) is traditionally spread on grilled bread, bread sticks, or a chunk of a crusty country loaf. But try it with goat cheese on Toasted Bread Rounds (see page 30) or with cold roast beef, or slather it on lamb chops just off the grill. Tapenade can be stored in the refrigerator for up to six months.

- ½ pound large, black Greek olives, pitted
- 1 ounce anchovy fillets
- 1 clove garlic, minced
- 2 tablespoons capers
- 2 tablespoons olive oil
  Black pepper to taste

1. Place olives in a food processor or blender. Add anchovies, garlic, capers, and olive oil; process or blend briefly. Mixture should be blended but still coarse. Transfer to a bowl and add black pepper to taste.

2. Spoon tapenade into a crock or jar and cover with a thin layer of olive oil.

Makes 1 cup.

SICILIAN TOMATO SPREAD

The Italians used to make tomato paste by leaving tomato sauce in the sun to dry out. The resultant paste was enjoyed as a snack, spread on bread. One of San Francisco's Italian restaurants serves a similar spread. It's disarmingly simple—tomato paste spruced up with garlic and fresh herbs—but remarkably tasty when slathered on bread sticks, Toasted Bread Rounds (see page 30), or a crusty Italian loaf. It will keep under oil, refrigerated, for a week.

- ½ cup tomato paste
- 1 teaspoon red wine vinegar
- 1 tablespoon olive oil
- ½ teaspoon chopped fresh thyme
- 1 large clove garlic, minced

Combine all ingredients thoroughly. Pack into a small crock. Serve immediately or cover with a thin film of olive oil and refrigerate.

Makes ½ cup.

ROASTED GARLIC CONFIT

Whenever you roast a duck or goose, freeze the fat that you trim away from the bird before roasting. When you've hoarded about 2 cups, render it to make this unctuous garlic *confit* (preserve). Garlic roasted slowly turns wonderfully creamy and mild—a delicious surprise to the uninitiated. Serve the confit with garlic Toasted Bread Rounds (see page 30) or Cocktail Scones (see page 30). It can be stored, covered with a layer of oil or fat, for months. Use leftover fat from the recipe to pan-fry potatoes, to cook an omelet, or to sauté croutons or mushrooms.

- 4 heads garlic
- 2 cups rendered duck or goose fat

1. Preheat oven to 200° F. Peel away the papery outer leaves of garlic but leave heads intact. Put them in a small, deep baking dish just large enough to hold them. Add the fat, which should completely cover the garlic. Roast until the garlic is extremely tender (about 1½ hours). Roasting time will depend on the age of the garlic.

2. Remove garlic from fat with a slotted spoon and let cool. Squeeze the cooked cloves from their skins and place them in a crock. Mash cloves with a wooden spoon handle, then cover the crock with a layer of olive oil or rendered fat. Refrigerate until ready to serve.

3. Remove confit from refrigerator 2 to 3 hours before serving to soften the fat. Remove top layer of fat or oil and spread mashed garlic on warm toasts. It is especially delicious with cream cheese or goat cheese.

Makes about 1½ cups.

MEDITERRANEAN EGGPLANT SPREAD

The warm flavors of the Mediterranean come through in this coarse eggplant spread, designed to be made in the food processor. Serve it with Onion-Bacon Scones (see page 30) or Cocktail Crumpets (see page 79) before a dinner of garlicky roast lamb or chicken. It can be stored in the refrigerator up to two weeks.

- 1 eggplant, about 1 pound
- ¼ cup olive oil
- 2 red bell peppers, chopped
- 2 large tomatoes, peeled, seeded, and chopped
- 1 medium zucchini, chopped
- 2 cloves garlic, minced
- 1 teaspoon paprika, preferably Hungarian
- 1 teaspoon ground cumin
  Juice of 1 lemon
  Salt to taste

1. Preheat oven to 450° F. Trim ends of eggplant; cut eggplant into lengthwise slices, about ¼ inch thick.

2. Brush a baking sheet with 2 tablespoons of the oil, then heat in oven for 5 minutes. Place eggplant slices on heated baking sheet and bake 10 to 15 minutes. Remove from oven and let cool.

3. Place eggplant in food processor and purée coarsely. Set aside.

4. In remaining 2 tablespoons oil, sauté peppers on medium heat for 7 to 8 minutes or until soft. Add the remaining ingredients and continue cooking 2 minutes. Remove from heat and cool slightly.

5. Combine pepper mixture and eggplant and process briefly. The spread should be very coarse. Pack into crocks and seal with a little olive oil.

6. At serving time, taste and adjust salt and lemon as necessary. Serve with crackers, warm pita bread, or leaves of Belgian endive.

Makes 2 cups.

IN A SUPPORTING ROLE...

What you put your pâté *on* is every bit as important as what you put in it. The item you choose for the supporting role should be delicious in itself; it should be sturdy enough to support the spread, and it should be either very subtly flavored, like a simple melba toast, or seasoned in such a way that it complements the main event—a garlic-rubbed Toasted Bread Round with Mediterranean Eggplant Spread (page 29), for example.

The three breads below can be made in advance, cooled, and frozen. No need to thaw—just reheat in a moderate oven on baking sheets.

COCKTAIL SCONES

These savory biscuits, made in a cocktail "mini" size, can be seasoned to order with herbs, cheese, nuts, or bacon. They make a delightful mouthful on their own, or you can halve them and add a filling: Split the scones and fill with sliced smoked beef and a dab of Tapenade (see page 29) for a hearty, pass-around hors d'oeuvre; add chopped fresh or dried dill to the dough, split and butter the scones, and fill with thinly sliced ham; fill scones with a thin slice of Quick Country Pâté (see page 24) and a swipe of good mustard.

2 cups unbleached flour
1 tablespoon baking powder
½ teaspoon baking soda
½ teaspoon salt
½ cup unsalted butter
1 egg
½ cup sweet wine such as cooking Sauterne or cream sherry
⅓ cup whipping cream
Additional cream

1. Preheat oven to 400° F. Stir together flour, baking powder, baking soda, and salt. Cut in butter until mixture resembles coarse crumbs. In a bowl, whisk together egg, wine, and the ⅓ cup cream. Add to dry ingredients and stir just to combine.

2. Turn dough out on a lightly floured surface and, with lightly floured hands, pat into a ½-inch-thick rectangle. (Dough will be sticky.) Cut out rounds with a small floured cookie cutter.

3. Brush tops of scones with a little additional cream and bake until golden (12 to 15 minutes).
Makes about 2 dozen scones.

Cheddar Scones Add ½ cup grated sharp Cheddar to the wine-egg mixture.

Walnut Scones Add ½ cup chopped walnuts (or pecans) to the wine-egg mixture.

Onion-Bacon Scones Sauté ⅓ cup minced onion in some bacon fat for about 10 minutes or until softened. Let cool, then add to wine-egg mixture.

TOASTED BREAD ROUNDS

This all-purpose "cracker" can be the basis for a dozen flights of fancy. You can make it from virtually any shape or type of bread—try rye or pumpernickel, for instance— but be sure to start with an honest, good-flavored loaf and one that's fairly dense in texture. Some airy commercial breads make fragile bread rounds filled with potholes.

To vary the bread rounds, use a little walnut or hazelnut oil in place of some of the olive oil; sprinkle rounds with freshly grated Parmesan cheese before baking; or add your choice of chopped herbs to the oil: thyme, rosemary, oregano, parsley, or *herbes de Provence.*

½ cup olive oil
2 tablespoons unsalted butter
2 garlic cloves, minced (optional)
1 long day-old French baguette or similar French-style bread

1. Preheat oven to 350° F. Heat oil and butter together with garlic (if used) until butter is melted. (The garlic can steep in the oil for several hours, if desired.)

2. With a sharp, serrated knife, cut the bread into ¼-inch-thick slices on the diagonal. Brush slices liberally on both sides with butter-oil mixture and place on a baking sheet.

3. Bake until golden (about 10 minutes).
Makes about 40 rounds.

HALLIE'S CORN CRACKERS

Thin and crisp and deliciously "corny," these crackers were inspired by cookbook author Maida Heatter. They make a fine hors d'oeuvre on their own with a bowl of mixed olives, or put them beside a crock of Tapenade (see page 29), a ham mousse, or thin slices of hot-pepper jack cheese. They can be stored up to one week in an airtight container.

2 cups sifted flour
2 teaspoons baking powder
½ teaspoon salt
½ cup unsalted butter, softened
2 tablespoons sugar
2 eggs, at room temperature
1 cup each milk and water
½ cup white cornmeal
½ teaspoon cayenne pepper or fennel seed (optional)

1. Preheat oven to 375° F. Sift together flour, baking powder, and salt. In large bowl of electric mixer, cream butter until light and fluffy. Add sugar and beat in eggs, one at a time.

2. Combine milk and water and add to egg-butter mixture alternately with flour mixture in 3 additions, using low speed. Mix in cornmeal. Force the mixture through a sieve.

3. Butter a 10½- by 15½-inch jelly roll pan. Heat in oven for 1 minute. Pour in ⅔ cup batter; tilt to coat bottom of pan evenly. Sprinkle with cayenne or fennel seed, if desired.

4. Bake 5 minutes, or until edges begin to curl and batter is firm enough to cut; cut into 16 squares. Continue baking until crackers are brown and crisp. Cool crackers on paper towels. Baking time will vary depending on the thickness of the crackers. Do not hesitate to remove some crackers from the oven before others.

5. Repeat 5 times with remaining batter.

Makes about 8 dozen crackers.

Toasted Bread Rounds and Cocktail Scones make tasty foundations for spreads and sliced meats, for chutneys and cheeses, or for simple herb butters. Here, bread rounds topped with a basil butter share the spotlight with ham-and-scone "sandwiches"; you can make the fluted edges with a cookie cutter.

VEGETABLES

Slowly, but steadily, the American vegetable marketplace is expanding. Vegetables that heretofore were exotic and hard to obtain are now almost commonplace, thanks to faster transport and a more sophisticated consumer. Okra, fennel, red bell peppers, celery root . . . You may not have grown up with these vegetables, but these days you can find them in their season in small markets across the nation.

In particular, we're experiencing the influence of a wave of Asian immigrants: Bean sprouts, bean curd, Japanese cucumbers, Chinese cabbage (bok choy), dried mushrooms, snow peas, and Japanese white radish (daikon) are now staples in many a supermarket. And if your produce department doesn't have the vegetable you need, ask for it. Chances are it's not hard to find.

It's all good news for the host or hostess, who can put together a tempting variety of vegetable-based hors d'oeuvres in *any* season. Guests who are watching their waistlines will appreciate an inviting assortment of crudités (see photograph on page 35). And *everyone* will appreciate having some tangy pickles or marinated vegetables to balance the party's heartier hors d'oeuvres.

Before a full-course dinner or lavish buffet, serve a light and piquant appetizer such as Giardiniera or Pickled Okra (at right). No point in filling your guests up on hors d'oeuvres when there's much more to come! But even when you're planning an all-hors d'oeuvres affair, a few lighter vegetable choices are always welcome.

GIARDINIERA

You can find *giardiniera*—garden vegetables in brine—in almost any Italian delicatessen, but making your own is an easy endeavor. Choose brilliantly colored produce from your garden or market, then combine the vegetables in the jar in a vivid mélange, or arrange them in neat layers of contrasting color. Either way, a seasonal giardiniera is a handsome production and an excellent partner to cocktails. Let it age one week before using; it will keep up to one year.

 5 *small carrots*
 1 *medium bunch celery*
 3 *medium zucchini*
 10 *pearl onions*
 3 *sweet red peppers*
 1 *cauliflower*
 8 *cups water*
 1¾ *cups white vinegar*
 ¼ *cup salt*
 ¼ *cup mustard seed*
 ½ *cup sugar*
 1 *teaspoon fennel seed*
 2 *two-inch strips of orange rind, all white pith removed*
 2 *two-inch strips of lemon rind, all white pith removed*
 6 *cloves garlic, peeled but not chopped*
 3 *small whole red chile peppers, fresh or dried*
 1 *cup black Greek olives, unpitted*

1. Peel carrots and cut into ¼-inch-thick strips no longer than the diameter of your canning jars. Trim celery and zucchini and cut into strips the same size as the carrots. Peel onions. Seed and derib peppers, then cut into ¼-inch-wide strips. Separate cauliflower into small flowerets.

2. In a large stockpot, bring water, vinegar, salt, mustard seed, sugar, fennel seed, orange rind, lemon rind, garlic, and chiles to a boil. Add all the prepared vegetables and cook 45 seconds. Drain vegetables, reserving liquid.

3. Return liquid to stock pot and simmer an additional 5 minutes. Arrange vegetables attractively in clean glass crocks or mason jars, putting a few olives at the bottom, middle, and top. Pour in hot brine and seal.
Makes 4 quarts.

PICKLED OKRA

A standby on the southern table, okra suffers—undeservedly—from lack of attention in other parts of the United States. This recipe should earn it some converts, for a good okra pickle is one of the handiest and tastiest treats a host can have in the pantry. Choose small, firm, unblemished pods and plan to use them right away. Once pickled, they can be eaten within a week or aged for up to a year. Serve with beer or iced tea at a picnic or barbecue, and follow with ribs or southern fried chicken, potato salad, and biscuits.

 8 *to 10 cloves garlic, peeled*
 4 *cups cider vinegar*
 2 *tablespoons dill seed*
 2 *tablespoons salt*
 2 *tablespoons mustard seed*
 2 *teaspoons sugar*
 4 *small fresh hot green chile peppers or 1 teaspoon dried hot red pepper flakes*
 2 *pounds okra*

1. In a large saucepan combine garlic cloves, vinegar, dill seed, salt, mustard seed, sugar, and chiles. Bring to a boil, then reduce heat to maintain a steady simmer. Simmer mixture 5 minutes. Remove from heat and cool completely.

2. Pack okra, untrimmed, into sterilized glass canning jars, small tips down, and pour the cooled brine over the okra. Seal jars. Place in boiling water bath and process 20 minutes.
Makes 4 pints.

You'll always be ready for drop-in guests with pantry shelves stocked with Giardiniera, a mosaic of garden vegetables pickled in a clear glass jar.

HOT AND TANGY ASIAN PICKLES

A delicious accompaniment to Vegetarian Egg Rolls (see page 37) or Garlic and Hot-Pepper Almonds (see page 14), these zippy cucumber pickles are a real appetite arouser. They do not need to age, but they can be made up to a week ahead. Cocktails, beer, or a fruity Chenin Blanc would be good companions.

- 3 pounds Japanese cucumbers (do not peel)
- 2 tablespoons salt
- 1 cup sesame oil
- 5 cloves garlic, minced
- 1 tablespoon dried hot red pepper flakes
- 1 tablespoon Szechuan brown peppercorns (available in Chinese markets)
  Grated rind of 2 oranges
- ¼ cup Japanese rice vinegar
- ¼ cup sugar
- 5 cloves garlic, peeled
  Rind of 1 orange, cut into ¼-inch strips, all white pith removed

1. Slice cucumbers in half lengthwise. Scoop out any seeds and slice into ¼-inch-thick half-rounds. Transfer to a large bowl, add salt, and set aside for 20 minutes. Drain cucumbers in colander.

2. In a large, deep skillet, heat ¾ cup of the oil over moderate heat. Add garlic, pepper flakes, peppercorns, and grated orange rind. Add drained cucumbers, toss quickly for 10 seconds and immediately add vinegar and sugar. Cook an additional 30 seconds, then remove from heat.

3. Pack cucumbers into a clean glass or plastic jar with a lid, alternating layers of cucumber with whole garlic cloves and orange rind. Top with remaining sesame oil and lid and refrigerate.

Makes about 5 cups.

MOROCCAN CARROTS

Paula Wolfert, a renowned authority on the cooking of Morocco, inspired this refreshing and colorful opener. If you use carrots with the fresh green tops still attached, the dish will be all the prettier. And there's no need to peel those young, tender carrots. Serve with Spicy Persian Lamb Balls (see page 61), Indonesian Chicken Skewers (see page 63), or Lime and Ginger Scallop Skewers (see page 45).

- 24 small whole fresh garden carrots with tops or 10 to 12 small storebought carrots, peeled and cut into 3-inch lengths
- 2 to 3 tablespoons lemon juice
- ½ cup olive oil
- 1 teaspoon brown sugar
- ⅛ teaspoon ground cinnamon
  Cayenne pepper and salt to taste

1. If carrot tops are fresh and green, leave them on. Bring a large pot of salted water to a boil, add carrots and parboil until just tender, about 3 to 4 minutes. Drain carrots and put them immediately in a bowl of ice water to stop the cooking and retain their color.

2. In a glass, ceramic, or stainless steel bowl, combine 2 tablespoons lemon juice, olive oil, sugar, cinnamon, and cayenne to taste. Whisk well. Drain carrots and pat dry. Transfer to a serving bowl and pour the dressing over them. Let marinate 15 minutes. Taste; add salt and adjust other seasonings as necessary.

Makes 2 dozen little carrot "bites."

WINTER CAPONATA, SICILIAN STYLE

Less well known than the familiar eggplant-tomato caponata but just as tasty is this winter version, which uses end-of-the-year produce such as anise and celery root. Serve it with garlicky Toasted Bread Rounds (see page 30) and Italian wine—a light-bodied red or a crisp, dry white.

- 10 ounces fresh spinach, cleaned and stems trimmed
- 1 small bulb sweet anise (fennel)
- 1 small celery root, peeled and diced
- 1 medium carrot, peeled and grated
- 3 tablespoons olive oil
- 1 large tomato, peeled, seeded, and chopped
- 1 tablespoon tomato paste
- 1 teaspoon sugar
- 2 tablespoons bread crumbs
- 2 tablespoons sweet pickle relish
- 1 tablespoon capers
  Salt and black pepper to taste

1. Cook spinach in a large pot over medium heat in just the water clinging to the leaves, stirring with a wooden spoon, until barely wilted, about 30 seconds. Drain well, then chop coarsely. Trim coarse outer leaves of fennel; dice. Parboil in boiling salted water for 5 minutes; drain. Parboil celery root in boiling salted water 3 minutes; drain. Parboil carrot in boiling salted water 1 minute; drain.

2. Heat oil in a large skillet over moderate heat. Add spinach, fennel, celery root, and carrot; sauté 3 to 4 minutes. Add tomato, tomato paste, and sugar; simmer 10 minutes. Add bread crumbs, relish, and capers; cook 3 minutes. Remove from heat and cool completely. Let "age" 2 days, then serve cool or at room temperature. At serving time, taste; adjust seasonings if necessary.

Makes about 4½ cups.

ZUCCHINI FRITTERS

A veritable garden of herbs goes into these fried zucchini rounds, which have the taste and look of summer. Follow them with a meal of Summer Specials: sliced ripe tomatoes, corn soup, grilled salmon, and fresh berries, plus a crisp California white wine.

    8 medium zucchini, grated
    1 carrot, peeled and grated
    3 cloves garlic, minced
    3 whole eggs plus 2 egg yolks
    5 green onions, minced
    2 tablespoons minced fresh dill
       or 1 tablespoon dried
    ¾ cup chopped parsley
    ½ cup fresh basil leaves
    2 tablespoons fresh tarragon or
       1 teaspoon dried
    ½ cup grated Jarlsberg or
       Gruyère cheese
    2 tablespoons lemon juice
       Salt and black pepper to taste
       Pinch cayenne pepper
    ¾ to 1 cup flour
    1 to 1½ cups peanut oil
       Crème fraîche or sour cream

1. In a blender or food processor, place zucchini, carrots, garlic, eggs and egg yolks, green onions, dill, parsley, basil, tarragon, cheese, lemon juice, salt, pepper, and cayenne. Process to blend well, then transfer to a large bowl. Add flour ¼ cup at a time until mixture holds together but is not "gluey."

2. Heat ¼ inch of the oil in a medium sauté pan. When oil is almost smoking, drop large spoonfuls of the batter into the pan. Flatten each round slightly, then sauté quickly, 30 to 45 seconds on each side. Drain fritters on paper towels and keep warm while you fry the remainder. Serve immediately, with a dollop of crème fraîche or sour cream.

Makes about 4 dozen fritters.

Crudités—raw fresh vegetables—are always welcome as part of an hors d'oeuvres buffet. Throughout the year, the produce market yields a varied palette of fresh vegetables. Choose the best the season has to offer, prepare them in bite-sized pieces, and arrange them in an eye-catching still life, with a dip or two alongside (see pages 37–39).

35

Sautéed Red Peppers

¼ cup olive oil

5 red bell peppers, halved, seeded, deribbed, and cut into thin strips

2 tablespoons minced fresh oregano or 1 tablespoon dried

3 cloves garlic, minced

Lay out prosciutto slices. Put 5 to 6 strips of Sautéed Red Peppers on each prosciutto slice, then roll each slice into a neat cylinder, with the tips of the peppers poking out at each end. Place rolls on a round plate, dust them with parsley, and serve. *Makes about 2 dozen prosciutto rolls.*

Sautéed Red Peppers Heat olive oil in a heavy skillet. When it is hot, add peppers and toss to coat all over with oil. Add the oregano and cook over moderate heat, half-covered, for 20 minutes. Add garlic and stir briskly for 30 seconds. Remove from heat and cool completely. Use immediately with prosciutto or store, in the cooking oil, covered, in refrigerator.

HOMEMADE POTATO CHIPS

Better than any store-bought chip, this homemade version is twice-fried for extra crispness. When you make them yourself, you *know* they're fresh, and you can adjust the salt to your liking. A welcome bonus: The potato skins, which can be buttered and baked until golden and crisp (see opposite page). Leave a little potato "flesh" on the skins when you peel them for best results.

3 large russet potatoes
    Peanut or corn oil for deep-frying
    Coarse salt

1. Peel potatoes. Reserve skins for Baked Potato Skins (at right), if desired. Slice potatoes ¼ inch thick and place in a bowl of ice water until ready to fry.

Sweet red peppers and thin-sliced prosciutto are a made-in-heaven match. Present these juicy bundles as part of an antipasto platter or include them in a summer buffet.

PROSCIUTTO AND RED PEPPERS

Paper-thin Italian ham wrapped around garlicky sautéed red bell peppers makes for a juicy but potentially messy little bundle, best eaten with a knife and fork. For finger food, nestle the bundles in endive leaves or on Toasted Bread Rounds (see page 30) cut on a long diagonal. Serve the prosciutto rolls with a dry Italian white wine or a dry California white Zinfandel.

⅓ pound prosciutto, sliced paper thin

1 tablespoon minced parsley

2. In a heavy skillet or deep fryer, heat at least 3 inches of oil to 375° F. Dry potatoes well between kitchen towels. Add potatoes to hot oil and fry until they are lightly golden. Drain on paper towels.

3. Raise the temperature of the oil to 400° F and refry the potatoes until very crisp and golden. (If you are doubling or tripling the recipe, do the second frying with fresh oil.) Drain on paper towels, salt lightly, and serve immediately.

Makes about 5 dozen chips.

BAKED POTATO SKINS

These buttery baked potato peels are worth making even if you don't have any plans for the potatoes! You can store the peeled potatoes in ice water for a day or two, then use them in any potato recipe. In the meantime, the crusty baked skins are utterly addicting, either on their own or with sour cream and caviar (see page 47).

> *Approximately 2 cups potato peelings, preferably with some potato "flesh" left on them*
> *2 tablespoons unsalted butter*

Preheat oven to 450° F. Place skins on a lightly oiled or buttered baking sheet. Dot with butter. Bake until skins are quite golden and crisp (about 20 minutes). Drain on paper towels and serve immediately.

Makes about 6 dozen potato "crisps."

VEGETARIAN EGG ROLLS

Packaged wonton skins, available in Chinese and many American markets, take the work out of making these deep-fried rolls. The colorful stuffing is studded with peanuts and laced with the mellow flavor of sesame oil. Serve them with Hot and Spicy Chinese Dipping Sauce (see page 38) and a California or Alsatian Gewürztraminer.

> *3 dried black Chinese mushrooms*
> *Peanut oil*
> *3 green onions, minced*
> *2 teaspoons minced fresh ginger*
> *1 teaspoon minced fresh garlic*
> *⅓ pound white button mushrooms, minced*
> *1 teaspoon sesame oil*
> *½ cup bean sprouts*
> *¼ cup grated carrots*
> *2 tablespoons chopped roasted peanuts*
> *1 package (1 dozen) wonton skins*
> *2 green onions, minced (optional)*

1. Soak dried mushrooms in warm water to cover for 30 minutes. Drain and squeeze excess moisture from mushrooms. Trim tough stems and dice caps.

2. Heat 2 tablespoons peanut oil in a large skillet. Add the 3 green onions, ginger, and garlic and cook 3 minutes over moderate heat. Add button mushrooms and continue cooking an additional 2 minutes. Add black mushrooms and cook 30 seconds. Remove from heat.

3. Stir in sesame oil, bean sprouts, carrots, and peanuts. Put about 2½ tablespoons filling on the bottom third of each wonton skin. Roll up and seal ends with water.

4. In a large wok or deep heavy skillet, heat at least 4 inches of peanut oil to 375° F. Fry egg rolls a few at a time until golden brown on all sides. Drain on paper towels. Cut each egg roll into thirds on the diagonal. Serve hot, with a garnish of minced green onion (if used).

Makes 3 dozen slices.

Make-Ahead Tip Skins can be stuffed and rolled a few hours ahead of time, then deep-fried just before serving.

DIPPING SAUCES

The wise party-giver knows that cocktail dips are more than just one half of that overworked duo, Chips and Dip. Indeed, they are far more versatile—suitable as toppings for skewered grilled foods (see pages 62–63), as sauces to partner a platter of cold sliced meats and a basket of breads (see page 59), or—yes—as dips, but with more imaginative "dippers" than the ubiquitous chips. Homemade Potato Chips (see opposite page), breadsticks, toasted triangles of pita bread, or a "still life" of the most colorful seasonal vegetables (see page 35) are good alternatives.

The sauces that follow are a varied lot with distinctive ethnic features that suggest the most compatible accompaniments: freshly fried tortilla chips would be right at home with Salsa Cruda but sorely out of place with a Provençal Anchoiade.

All these sauces, with the exception of the salsa, can be made at least a day ahead, although their flavors can change subtly as they sit. Adjust seasoning just before serving.

BOUCHERON DIP

Goat cheese adds its distinctive tang to this creamy dip, to accompany a colorful basket full of artichoke hearts, mushrooms, red and green peppers, and hearts of romaine.

> *1 cup plain yogurt*
> *2 ounces Boucheron cheese or other mild fresh goat cheese*
> *¼ cup sour cream*
> *1 tablespoon minced fresh herbs, for garnish (chives, dill, thyme, or chervil, for example)*

1. Line a sieve with cheesecloth and set it over a bowl. Spoon yogurt into sieve and let drain two hours.

2. Force the Boucheron through a coarse strainer. Stir in drained yogurt and the sour cream. Garnish with fresh minced herbs of choice.

Makes approximately 1¼ cups.

ANCHOIADE

A smooth and pungent spread enjoyed in southern France and Corsica, *anchoiade* is slathered on toasted French bread, pizza doughs, and breadsticks. Try it on Toasted Bread Rounds (see page 30) or Cocktail Crumpets (see page 79) baked briefly, or use it as a spread on miniature egg-salad sandwiches. It keeps, refrigerated, for up to three weeks and should be served with cocktails or a dry white wine.

> 6 tins (2 oz each) oil-packed anchovies
> 3 cloves garlic, minced
> ½ cup minced parsley
> 3 egg yolks
> 1½ cups fresh bread crumbs
> ¼ cup red wine vinegar
> ¾ cup olive oil
> 1 tablespoon minced fresh thyme (do not substitute dried thyme)

1. In a blender combine anchovies with their oil, garlic, parsley, and egg yolks. Blend well. Add bread crumbs and blend. Mixture will be a thick paste. Add red wine vinegar and blend.

2. With blender on low speed, add olive oil drop by drop. Mixture will mount like a mayonnaise. Transfer Anchoiade to a bowl and stir in fresh thyme.
Makes about 3 cups.

HOT AND SPICY CHINESE DIPPING SAUCE

This fiery blend makes an uncommonly good dip for a variety of hot and cold foods, and it can be toned down or punched up at will. Serve it with grilled skewered chicken, mushrooms, or bean curd; with raw hearts of Chinese cabbage and lightly steamed carrot spears; with slices of cool cucumber or daikon (Japanese white radish); and with cold boiled shrimp or crab.

> 2 cloves garlic, minced
> 1 tablespoon rice wine
> ½ to 1 teaspoon hot chili paste (available in Chinese markets) or ⅛ teaspoon dried hot red pepper flakes
> 1 tablespoon chili sauce
> 2 tablespoons sesame oil
> 1 teaspoon sugar
> 1 tablespoon minced green onion
> 2 tablespoons chicken stock
> 1 teaspoon minced ginger
> 2 tablespoons soy sauce, or more to taste

Combine all ingredients in a small saucepan and simmer 2 minutes. Cool and refrigerate for up to 4 days.
Makes about ½ cup.

GREEK CUCUMBER SAUCE WITH SPINACH AND DILL

This wonderfully tart concoction somehow captures all the flavors of Greek cooking in a single bowl. Serve it with skewers of grilled lamb or salmon; with raw tomatoes, zucchini and mushrooms; or with Spicy Persian Lamb Balls (see page 61).

> 2 cucumbers, peeled, seeded, and coarsely chopped
> 1½ teaspoons salt
> ½ yellow onion, peeled and coarsely chopped
> ½ cup whole-milk plain yogurt
> 1 tablespoon lemon juice
> 1 tablespoon minced fresh dill or ½ tablespoon dried
> ¼ cup chopped raw spinach
> 2 tablespoons olive oil
> Cayenne pepper to taste
> Salt and black pepper to taste
> 1 green onion, minced
> 1 teaspoon minced fresh oregano

1. Combine cucumbers and salt in a bowl. Stir well, then let sit for 1 hour. Drain off all liquid and transfer cucumbers to a clean bowl.

2. In a blender combine onion, yogurt, lemon juice, dill, and spinach. Blend well, then transfer to a bowl and whisk in olive oil, cayenne, salt, and pepper; stir in green onion and oregano. Taste and adjust seasonings if necessary. The mixture should be tart and aggressively flavored. Add cucumbers and let stand 45 minutes. Taste again and add more seasoning if necessary. Refrigerate until serving time.
Makes about 1½ cups.

SALSA CRUDA

This basic uncooked salsa is found on the table of practically every restaurant in Mexico. It is an indispensable presence at a Mexican meal and should be a part of any Mexican-themed collation. Set it out as a dip for fried tortilla chips or as a sauce for grilled or broiled seafood. It is delightful spooned onto raw oysters or steamed mussels on the half shell; or try it wrapped up in a warm soft tortilla with crispy Carnitas (see page 56) or Pork in Green Chile (see page 58).

> 1 yellow onion, peeled and minced
> 3 fresh ripe tomatoes, peeled, seeded, and coarsely chopped
> 2 tablespoons minced cilantro
> 1 clove garlic, minced
> 1 small fresh green chile pepper, minced, or more to taste
> 1 tablespoon lime juice
> Salt to taste

Prepare all ingredients. Combine in a small bowl no more than an hour before serving. Do not add salt until the last minute. Salsa is best when freshly made.
Makes about ¾ cup.

CURRY SAUCE

A smooth and silky curry dip works magic on hard-cooked eggs, boiled shrimp and crab, a basket of snow peas and hearts of bok choy, or a platter of cold cuts. Or serve it with thinly sliced cold chicken, smoked turkey, roast pork or ham, and an assortment of premium breads. The sauce keeps up to two weeks, refrigerated.

> ¼ cup honey
> 1 cup chicken stock
> 1 ounce (2 tablespoons) hot curry powder
> 1 tablespoon ground coriander
> ½ teaspoon cayenne pepper
> ½ teaspoon white pepper
> ⅓ cup Dijon mustard
> 3⅓ cups mayonnaise, preferably homemade

1. Combine honey and chicken stock in a small saucepan. Heat and stir until honey dissolves. Add curry powder, coriander, cayenne, and white pepper. Continue cooking over moderate heat until mixture is reduced to ¾ cup.

2. Remove from heat and cool completely. Add mustard and mayonnaise. Mix well.

Makes about 4 cups.

WATERCRESS DIP WITH GREEN ONIONS AND BASIL

This dip is a showstopper—a nutty, coarse-textured creation fragrant with basil and brilliantly green. Arrange a basket of crudités beside it: cherry tomatoes, cauliflower and broccoli flowerets, snow peas, endive leaves, zucchini and carrot spears, artichoke hearts, radishes or fennel. It keeps up to 10 days, refrigerated.

> 3 cups watercress, stems trimmed
> ¾ cup fresh small basil leaves
> ¼ cup minced garlic
> ½ cup good-quality olive oil

> 1 cup freshly grated Parmesan cheese
> ¾ cup whipping cream
> ½ cup finely ground walnuts
> ¼ cup minced green onions
> Salt and freshly ground black pepper to taste
> 1 tablespoon milk or water (optional)

1. In a blender combine watercress, basil, garlic, olive oil, and Parmesan. Blend until pasty. Add cream and blend only until mixed; do not overblend.

2. Transfer mixture to a bowl and stir in walnuts and green onion. Add salt and pepper to taste. Mixture will thicken as it stands; if desired, add a tablespoon of milk or water to thin it out before serving.

Makes 2 cups.

An appealing and unusual dip is the finishing touch to a basket of crudités, an assortment of steamed shellfish, or a platter of grilled skewered meats. Shown above are three selections from the recipes beginning on page 37: Boucheron Dip (top), Watercress Dip With Green Onions and Basil (left), and Curry Sauce (right).

FISH AND SHELLFISH

The watchwords of today's entertaining are "keep it light, keep it simple," and caterers—who are in the business of party-giving—report more interest in fish and shellfish than ever before. Many are staging cocktail parties with elaborate seafood bars and sushi bars (and elaborate fees to match!); "walkaway" seafood cocktails—in tiny sake cups or lettuce leaves—are extremely popular. Perhaps it's the increased concern for health and diet; perhaps it's the increased availability of quality seafood nationwide. Whatever the reason, fish and shellfish are more and more often the stars of the party.

Several of the appetizers below are based on raw seafood—sometimes "cooked" in citrus juice, sometimes not cooked at all. Although some guests may need convincing (in which case, give them some tempting alternatives), raw or barely cooked seafood makes a thoroughly appetizing hors d'oeuvre. And for those cooks with more money than time, fresh seafood is the easiest option. Set out a platter of chilled scallops, raw or steamed; oysters or clams on the half-shell; steamed mussels or clams, hot or cold; steamed or grilled prawns, hot or cold; crab claws, tiny bay shrimp, or lobster; and one or more of the marvelous shellfish sauces on pages 50-51. You won't have leftovers!

POTTED SHRIMP

The English often put potted shrimp on their tea tables, alongside a basket of warm or toasted brown bread. This savory spread also has an affinity for Champagne and cocktails, for thin-sliced rye bread, and warm Toasted Bread Rounds (see page 30). Substitute dill, chives, parsley, mint, or chervil for the tarragon, if desired. Make the mixture by hand or in a food processor; a blender makes too fine a paste.

2 pounds tiny cooked shrimp
1½ cups unsalted butter, at room temperature
1 tablespoon salt
1 teaspoon freshly ground black pepper
1 tablespoon lemon juice, or more to taste
1 tablespoon minced fresh tarragon

In a food processor fitted with the steel blade, process shrimp until they are coarsely chopped. Add butter, salt, pepper, lemon juice, and tarragon, and process until fairly smooth. Pack into 1-cup crocks, cover with plastic wrap or waxed paper, and refrigerate up to 2 weeks. *To make by hand*, chop shrimp very finely. Transfer to a bowl and work in softened butter, salt, pepper, lemon juice, and tarragon, blending well with the back of a wooden spoon.

Makes 3 cups.

COCONUT-MARINATED FISH

A bowl of firm-fleshed fish steeped in coconut milk and lime juice can be a dangerous thing. One taste, and duty flies out the window, replaced by dreams of white sands and cool surf. Serve this cool, clean-tasting concoction in lettuce "cups."

3 pounds firm fish fillets (salmon, halibut, sea bass, tuna)
1½ cups coconut milk (available frozen in Hispanic markets)
1½ cups fresh lime juice
3 tomatoes, peeled, seeded, and coarsely chopped
1 cup minced green onions, both green and white parts
½ cup sweet red bell pepper, in ¼-inch cubes
1 tablespoon kosher salt
¼ cup chopped parsley

Cut fish fillets into ½-inch cubes. In a large stainless steel, glass, or ceramic bowl, combine with coconut milk, lime juice, tomatoes, green onions, red pepper, salt, and parsley. Cover and marinate, refrigerated, 2 to 3 hours. Remove from refrigerator and let stand 15 minutes before serving.

Serves 10.

MARINATED SQUID

Squid rings (and the chopped tentacles, if you wish) poached with hot red pepper flakes, then bathed in a lemony vinaigrette, make a cool and refreshing opening for a Mexican or Italian meal. Serve them as part of an antipasto buffet or platter, or mound them in lettuce "cups" or fingers of Belgian endive.

3 pounds cleaned squid
½ cup dry white wine
¼ to ½ teaspoon dried hot red pepper flakes
4 small garlic cloves, peeled
½ cup parsley sprigs
¼ cup lemon juice
2 tablespoons red wine vinegar
1 cup minced red onion
½ cup olive oil
½ cup minced parsley
Salt to taste

1. Remove squid tentacles. If desired, cut into small pieces and combine with squid bodies, or reserve for another use. Cut squid bodies into rings ½ inch wide.

2. Place squid in a pot with wine, pepper flakes, garlic, and parsley sprigs. Add just enough water to cover. Bring to a boil. When water just boils, cover pot and remove from heat. Let squid cool in liquid.

3. Transfer cooled squid to a stainless steel, glass, or ceramic bowl; add lemon juice, vinegar, onion, and oil. Stir to blend. Just before serving, add minced parsley and salt to taste.

Serves 12 to 15.

A refreshing, light hors d'oeuvre, sushi (see page 48) is impressive but not all that difficult for a cook with a sharp knife and a steady hand.

CURRIED CRAB IN TINY CREAM PUFFS

Crab and curry, bound with a reduction of shallots and cream, make an excellent marriage. For a cocktail nibble, spoon the mixture into miniature cream puffs.

- 2 tablespoons unsalted butter
- ¼ cup minced shallots
- 2 cups whipping cream
- ¼ cup dry vermouth
- 1½ teaspoons hot curry powder, or more to taste
  Salt and freshly ground black pepper to taste
- ½ teaspoon lemon juice
- ¾ pound fresh cooked crabmeat
- 24 small cream puffs (see Pâte à Choux, page 70), split in half
  Chutney (optional)

1. In a medium skillet over moderate heat, melt butter and sauté shallots until soft but not brown. Add cream, bring to a boil, and add vermouth. Reduce mixture over high heat to 1 cup. Add curry powder, salt, pepper, and lemon juice. Taste; adjust seasoning as necessary. Mixture should be spicy.

2. Cool slightly; fold in crabmeat. Fill bottom half of cream puffs with crab mixture. Either dot with chutney (if used) or top with upper half.

Makes 2 dozen puffs.

SEVICHE

Seviche loses its zip when made more than 8 or 10 hours ahead; for best results, don't add salt until just before serving. Nestle spoonfuls in soft lettuce "cups," or set a bowl of seviche beside a basket filled with warm corn tortillas.

- 2 pounds firm white fish: cod, halibut, or snapper
- 2 small, firm cucumbers, diced
- 1 green bell pepper, cut into ¼-inch cubes
- 1 red bell pepper, cut into ¼-inch cubes
- 4 tomatoes, peeled, seeded, and finely chopped
- 2 small red onions, thinly sliced
- 4 green onions, both green and white parts, finely minced
- 2 jalapeño chiles, minced, or to taste
- ¼ cup each minced fresh basil, minced parsley, and minced cilantro
  Juice of 2 lemons and 3 limes
- ¼ cup olive oil
  Salt and freshly ground black pepper to taste
  Lettuce leaves
  Lemon and lime wedges, for garnish
  Cilantro sprigs, for garnish

In a large stainless steel, glass, or ceramic bowl, combine fish, cucumbers, green and red peppers, tomatoes, red and green onions, chiles, basil, parsley, cilantro, lemon and lime juice, and olive oil. Toss to mix thoroughly. Refrigerate at least 1½ hours but no more than 12 hours. Season to taste with salt and pepper just before serving. Serve on lettuce leaves, garnished with lemon and lime wedges and sprigs of cilantro.

Serves 12 generously.

TEA-SMOKED SHRIMP

The venerable Chinese art of tea-smoking lends a magnificent sweet, smoky character to shrimp in a matter of minutes. Serve the shrimp in their shells with plenty of napkins. A California or Alsatian Gewürztraminer would be a delicious partner.

- 5 pounds large raw shrimp (12 to 16 per pound)
- ½ cup soy sauce
- ½ cup rice wine
- ½ cup thinly sliced fresh ginger
- 5 cloves garlic, thinly sliced
- ½ cup jasmine tea leaves
- ¼ cup dark brown sugar
- ½ cup white rice
  Grated rind of 1 lemon and 1 orange

1. Place shrimp in a large stainless steel, glass, or ceramic bowl and add soy sauce, rice wine, ginger, and garlic. Cover and marinate, refrigerated, overnight.

2. Line a wok or heavy skillet with heavy-duty aluminum foil. Combine tea leaves, sugar, rice, and lemon and orange rinds. Place in wok or skillet atop the foil. Adjust a rack inside the wok or skillet to sit 1½ inches above the tea leaf mixture. Turn heat to high. Place shrimp on rack. When mixture begins to smoke, cover wok or skillet tightly with lid or with more foil. Smoke 5 minutes. Remove from heat and let rest, covered, for an additional 5 minutes. Serve warm or chilled.

Serves 20.

LITTLE CRAB CAKES

A creamy mixture of mustard-laced crabmeat sautéed in small "cakes" makes an elegant hors d'oeuvre, requiring Champagne or a dry white wine and some last-minute attention. You can make the crab mixture two hours ahead, but the sautéing must be done just before serving.

- 2 eggs
- ¼ cup each mayonnaise and flour
- ½ cup plus 2 tablespoons minced parsley
- 1 tablespoon dry mustard
- 1 teaspoon Dijon mustard
  Salt and freshly ground black pepper to taste
- 2 pounds fresh cooked crabmeat
  Worcestershire sauce to taste
  Oil for sautéing
  Kosher salt

1. In a medium bowl whisk eggs into mayonnaise. Stir in flour, ½ cup of the parsley, dry mustard, Dijon mustard, salt, and pepper. Fold in crabmeat. Taste and add Worcestershire as desired.

2. In a large skillet over moderately high heat, heat a thin film of oil. When oil is almost smoking, drop in the batter. Cakes can be any size; a scant ¼ cup is a good measure. Flatten cakes slightly and cook until golden, about 2 minutes on each side. Drain on paper towels and sprinkle with kosher salt and 2 tablespoons minced parsley. Serve immediately.

Makes about 2 dozen cakes.

DEVILED MUSSELS

Be careful not to overcook mussels when you steam them, for they will cook again in the oven to brown the bread crumbs. Serve very hot, with cocktails, Sauvignon Blanc, or a French Muscadet.

> 8 *pounds small mussels*
> 1 *cup each water and dry white wine*
> 1 *cup unsalted butter*
> ½ *cup each minced onion, minced red bell pepper, minced green bell pepper, and minced celery*
> ¼ *cup minced green onion*
> 2 *tablespoons Dijon mustard Salt and cayenne pepper to taste*
> ½ *cup fresh bread crumbs*

1. Preheat oven to 400°F. Scrub mussels well, pull out beard, and put in a large pot with the water and wine. Cover tightly; steam over high heat until mussels just open. Remove from heat. When mussels are cool enough to handle, remove from shells, reserving half the shells.

2. In a medium skillet over moderate heat, melt ½ cup butter. Add onion, red and green pepper, celery, and green onion. Sauté until vegetables are slightly softened, about 5 minutes. Stir in mustard. Add mussels, salt, and cayenne. Remove from heat.

3. Place one mussel and a little of the seasoned vegetable mixture in each mussel shell. Sprinkle with bread crumbs; dot with remaining butter. Bake until bread crumbs are well browned, 5 to 8 minutes.

Serves 12 generously.

A mustardy bread crumb-and-vegetable topping puts the "devil" in these Deviled Mussels. Broiled briefly to crisp the topping, the mussels should be served piping hot.

Scallops in a spicy cumin-cream dressing can be a first course, or, at a casual outdoor party, pass smaller portions nestled in soft lettuce cups, to be wrapped up and eaten taco-style. There's something immensely appealing about edible "packages," especially ones as light and lively as these. Margaritas make a good partner.

WARM SHELLFISH ANTIPASTO

From Ragusa, Sicily, comes this unusual, multilayered antipasto: crisp toast, shallot purée, cream-bound crabmeat, and a mantle of bread crumbs. Preparation entails several steps, but it's well worth the effort, and much of it can be done ahead. Scallops, shrimp, or lobster can substitute for the crabmeat. Serve with a dry Italian white wine or a sparkling wine.

 16 *Toasted Bread Rounds (see page 30)*
 ¼ *cup Dijon mustard*
 ½ *cup unsalted butter*
 5 *shallots, minced*
 ½ *cup white wine*
  Salt and pepper to taste
 1 *cup fresh bread crumbs*
 1½ *cups whipping cream*
 2 *cloves garlic, minced*
 2 *ounces (1 can) anchovies, very finely minced*
 2 *tablespoons lemon juice*
 3 *tablespoons finely minced parsley*
 1 *pound fresh crabmeat, cooked*
  Chopped chives or parsley, for garnish

1. Preheat oven to 400° F. Spread Toasted Bread Rounds with a thin film of mustard and set aside. In a small skillet over moderate heat, melt ¼ cup of the butter. Add half of the shallots and sauté for 2 to 3 minutes, until softened but not browned. Add wine, reduce heat to low, and cook until wine has evaporated completely, about 20 minutes. Season to taste with salt and pepper. Set aside.

2. In a medium skillet over moderately high heat, melt remaining butter. Add bread crumbs and toast quickly. When bread crumbs are crisp and browned, remove from heat and set aside.

3. In a small saucepan over moderately high heat, heat cream. Add remaining shallots and the garlic. Reduce cream by half. Add anchovies, lemon juice, and parsley.

4. To assemble, spread each Toasted Bread Round with a little of the sautéed shallot mixture; top with 2 tablespoons crab, a little of the cream-and-anchovy sauce, and a sprinkle of toasted crumbs. Bake until bubbly and toasted, about 5 to 8 minutes. Serve immediately, garnished with chopped chives.

Makes 16.

SCALLOPS ON A BED OF CUMIN CREAM

Crisp lettuce filled with spicy crème fraîche and lime-marinated scallops makes an intriguing bundle of contrasts. Serve these scallops with Carnitas (see page 56) and Tartitas Aztecas (see page 81) as part of a south-of-the-border buffet, or present them as a first course with a plate, knife, and fork.

> 1 pound fresh bay or sea scallops
> 2 tablespoons lime juice
> 2 tablespoons olive oil
> 2 tablespoons minced cilantro
> Salt and cayenne pepper to taste
> 1¼ cups crème fraîche or sour cream
> 1 teaspoon ground cumin, or more to taste
> 1 teaspoon lemon juice
> ½ teaspoon salt
> White pepper to taste
> 15 butter lettuce "cups"
> 2 tablespoons minced chives

1. Cut large scallops into ¼-inch cubes; leave small ones whole. Put scallops in a stainless steel, glass, or ceramic bowl along with lime juice, olive oil, cilantro, and salt and cayenne to taste. Cover. Marinate, refrigerated, up to 10 hours.

2. In a small bowl combine crème fraîche, cumin, lemon juice, and the ½ teaspoon salt. Season to taste with white pepper. To serve, arrange lettuce "cups" on a serving platter and put a heaping tablespoon of seasoned cream in each cup. Top with scallops and garnish with minced chives. Serve cool but not cold.

Serves 15.

LIME AND GINGER SCALLOP SKEWERS

Here's a no-cook appetizer for hot summer nights. The tangy marinade "cooks" the scallops, imparting hints of lime and ginger in the process.

> 6 tablespoons soy sauce
> 6 tablespoons lime juice
> 2 tablespoons minced fresh ginger
> 2 tablespoons minced green onion
> 3 tablespoons olive oil
> 1 tablespoon sesame oil
> 2 teaspoons minced garlic
> 1 tablespoon minced fresh horseradish or 2 tablespoons prepared horseradish
> 1 teaspoon hot chili oil (optional)
> ¼ cup minced cilantro
> 1 pound fresh scallops, cut into ⅓-inch cubes if large

1. In a large stainless, glass, or ceramic bowl combine soy sauce, lime juice, ginger, green onion, olive oil, sesame oil, garlic, horseradish, chili oil (if used), and cilantro. Mix well. Add scallops, toss to coat well with marinade, then cover and refrigerate 12 hours.

2. Thread 6- to 8-inch bamboo skewers with scallops and serve immediately or refrigerate for up to 3 hours. Scallops taste best when they are cold but not chilled.

Makes 2 dozen cocktail skewers.

SAKE CLAMS

For seafood lovers, few things are more appealing than a platter of steamed clams on the half-shell. These clams have been soaked with cornmeal (which prompts them to release any interior grit), then steamed with sake (Japanese rice wine) for exotic flavor. A pungent paste of *wasabi* (Japanese horseradish) and soy sauce can be dabbed on top, although more timid palates may prefer the soy sauce alone.

> 24 small fresh clams, tightly closed
> 2 tablespoons cornmeal
> ½ cup Japanese sake
> 1 tablespoon wasabi (available powdered in Japanese markets)
> ¼ cup water
> Soy sauce

1. Place clams in a stainless steel, glass, or ceramic bowl and add water to cover. Stir in cornmeal and let sit in refrigerator at least 3 hours. Drain and rinse clams, washing off any additional outer dirt.

2. Place clams and sake in a stainless steel pot and bring to a boil. Cover and steam until clams just open. Remove from heat and cool. Remove clams from shell, reserving half the shell. Replace clam in half-shell, arrange on a platter, and serve immediately, or refrigerate (remove platter from refrigerator 1 hour before serving).

3. Make a paste of wasabi and the water. Dot half the clams with a tiny bit of wasabi paste and brush with soy sauce; brush remaining clams with soy sauce only.

Serves 8.

BRANDADE

Dried salt cod is a virtual stranger to most American cooks, although in Europe its charms have long been known. Look for it in Italian or Scandinavian markets for use in this unctuous, garlicky spread from southern France. You'll need to start the recipe two days ahead, as the salt cod has to soak. Serve Brandade warm in a chafing dish, with homemade bread or Toasted Bread Rounds (see page 30).

- 1 piece (1¼ pounds) boneless and skinless salt cod
- 1 cup milk
- 2 garlic cloves, minced
- ⅓ cup cooked, mashed potato
- ½ cup olive oil
- 1 cup safflower oil
- ½ cup warm whipping cream
- 1½ tablespoons lemon juice Freshly ground black pepper to taste

1. Put cod in a large bowl and cover with water. Let it soak 36 hours at cool room temperature, changing water 4 times the first day. The second day change the water once and add the milk to the fresh water. When it has soaked at least an hour, drain fish well.

2. Put cod in a saucepan with water to cover. Bring to a boil, reduce heat to maintain a simmer, and simmer gently until fish is fully cooked, about 20 minutes. Drain. When fish is cool enough to handle, flake it, removing any bones or skin.

3. Place cod and garlic in food processor fitted with steel blade. Blend well. Add potato and process again. With motor running, add oils in a steady thin stream. Add cream all at once and process. Season with lemon juice and pepper.

Makes 4 cups.

Make-Ahead Tip Brandade can be made a day ahead, cooled, and refrigerated. Reheat slowly in a double boiler, thinning with warm cream if necessary.

HALLIE'S CHINESE SEVICHE

Marinating seafood in citrus to "cook" it is a concept with countless possibilities. Here, Chinese ingredients give seviche an Asian flavor. Serve it in tender lettuce "cups," with cocktails or white wine; substitute shrimp or a firm-fleshed white fish if you can't find the scallops.

- 2 pounds fresh sea scallops, cut into quarter-sized rounds, or 2 pounds small bay scallops, left whole
- ¾ cup soy sauce
- ½ cup fresh lime juice
- ¼ cup freshly grated horseradish
- ½ teaspoon dried hot red pepper flakes
- 1 tablespoon olive oil
- 1 teaspoon sesame oil
- 1 tablespoon minced garlic
- ½ cup minced water chestnuts
- ¼ cup chopped cilantro

Place scallops in a stainless steel, glass, or ceramic bowl. Stir in soy sauce, lime juice, horseradish, red pepper flakes, oils, garlic, water chestnuts, and half the cilantro. Let stand 10 minutes; or cover and refrigerate up to 12 hours. Add remaining cilantro just before serving.

Serves 20.

DRUNKEN SHRIMP

When you can find good, fresh-caught shrimp, there's no reason to fuss. Bake them briefly, then marinate them simply, in lemon, oil, garlic, parsley, and onion. Make as many as your budget allows: No one ever gets enough of these! A basket of crusty bread is useful to soak up the good tangy juices.

- 5 pounds jumbo shrimp (12 to 16 per pound)
  About ¼ cup olive oil
- 4 lemons, thinly sliced
- 3 tablespoons minced garlic
- ½ cup minced parsley
- 3 red onions, thinly sliced
  Salt

1. Preheat oven to 400° F. Place shrimp on a baking sheet. Brush with olive oil to coat. Bake until shrimp turn a brilliant pink but are still tender and moist, 5 to 9 minutes.

2. Put lemon slices in a stainless steel, glass, or ceramic bowl. Add any remaining olive oil, garlic, parsley, onions, and salt to taste. Add shrimp and toss well to coat. Cover and marinate, refrigerated, at least 6 hours or overnight. Serve at room temperature.

Serves about 20, with other appetizers.

SEAFOOD TARTARE

Steak Tartare has long been a presence on French restaurant menus, but Seafood Tartare is new—and very popular. Finely chopped and well-seasoned fish (*fresh* fish only!) makes a thoroughly refreshing—and low-calorie—appetizer, spooned onto crackers or lettuce leaves. You can use any firm-fleshed white fish, and you can substitute dill, chervil, or cilantro for some of the parsley. Serve with cocktails, sparkling wine, or a Sauvignon Blanc.

- 2 pounds firm white fish such as halibut or cod
- 2 white onions, finely minced
- 3 cloves garlic, finely minced
- 1 cup minced parsley
  Grated rind of 2 lemons
- ¼ cup lemon juice
- ½ cup olive oil
- 2 teaspoons kosher salt
  Freshly ground black pepper to taste
- ½ cup minced green onions, for garnish

Chop fish medium-fine by hand. Put in a stainless steel, glass, or ceramic bowl. Add onions, garlic, parsley, lemon rind, lemon juice, olive oil, salt, and pepper. Toss to combine. Cover and refrigerate 2 hours, or put in a serving bowl, garnish with green onions, and serve at once.

Makes 6 cups.

CAVIAR FOR THE BUDGET-CONSCIOUS

Serving good sturgeon caviar at a cocktail party is out of the question for most hosts and hostesses. Some people "compromise" by buying inexpensive lumpfish, but although it may *look* like the real thing, it is salty and indelicate and only serves to remind its eaters of what they're missing. Others may splurge on a little of the good stuff but have to spread it so thin that *no* one gets to enjoy it. Such economy combined with extravagance brings to mind the legendary Colette, who flatly stated (speaking of truffles), "If I can't have too many, I'll do without."

Now there's a better way. The "golden caviar" of Great Lakes whitefish is being sold across the country, and at very reasonable prices relative to its quality. These tiny golden eggs not only look good but taste good if they've been well cared for.

Most golden caviar is flash-frozen after processing; otherwise, the eggs get soggy and collapse almost immediately. When you buy it, it should still be frozen, or you should ask how long it has been out of the freezer. (Some markets take a tin or so out of the freezer each day to display on ice.) Don't buy a tin that has been out of the freezer more than a day.

Ideally, caviar should be stored at 28° F, which is colder than a refrigerator, but not as cold as most home freezers. So when you get your caviar home, fill a bowl with ice, nestle the tin in the ice, and set the bowl in the coldest part of the refrigerator. (Make sure no water can seep into the tin.) Then serve it within a day or two.

You can serve golden caviar just as you would black caviar. The only difference is that you don't have to scrimp!

☐ Spread it on warm buttered toast and serve with lemon.

☐ Spoon liberally onto blini (see page 75) with sour cream.

☐ Serve slices of small boiled potatoes topped with sour cream and caviar.

☐ Spoon a dollop of sour cream and some caviar atop crêpes flavored with dill (see page 98).

☐ Spoon a little onto raw oysters on the half-shell.

☐ Fill tiny Cream Puffs (see page 70) with sour cream, caviar, and chopped chives.

Golden whitefish caviar is an affordable luxury. Shown here atop crêpes (see page 22) with a dollop of sour cream, it can be served in any way you'd use good sturgeon caviar.

SPICE-FRIED HALIBUT

Looks are deceiving. Who would suspect these little halibut cubes would pack such a punch? But an overnight stay in chili powder and garlic gives them a fiery finish, best doused with an icy beer or a margarita. Bruce Aidells, a Berkeley, California, cooking teacher, provided the inspiration for this dish, which can be made completely ahead except for the final brief frying. Any firm-fleshed white fish, such as sea bass, rock cod, or swordfish, could substitute for the halibut.

  2 tablespoons red wine vinegar
  2 teaspoons minced garlic
  ½ teaspoon ground bay leaf
  1 tablespoon chili powder
    Salt and freshly ground black pepper to taste
  1 pound halibut fillets
    Corn oil for deep-frying
  ⅓ cup flour
    Minced parsley, for garnish
    Lemon wedges, for garnish

1. In a blender or food processor, place vinegar, garlic, bay leaf, and chili powder. Blend to a smooth paste. Transfer to a bowl and add salt and pepper to taste. (The amount of salt and pepper required depends on the freshness of the chili powder. Mixture should be highly spiced.)

2. Cut halibut into 16 cubes and marinate it in the paste overnight, covered, in the refrigerator.

3. Heat oil to 375° F in a deep-fryer or deep, heavy pot. Dust fish with flour, then deep-fry quickly until golden. Drain on paper towels and serve immediately, dusted with parsley and garnished with lemon wedges.

Makes 16 pieces.

NIGIRI SUSHI

Although it takes many years to become a full-fledged sushi chef, any cook with a sharp knife can make a modest platter of *nigiri sushi*. *Nigiri* are thin slices of raw fish draped across "fingers" of molded sushi rice. Tuna and shrimp both lend themselves to this treatment. See the photos opposite for guidance in making sushi. Accompany sushi with warm sake (Japanese rice wine), a dry white wine, or cocktails, and serve it soon after making it.

  1 tablespoon wasabi (Japanese horseradish, available powdered in Japanese markets)
  2 tablespoons rice vinegar
  1 cup water
  1½ pounds fresh tuna fillet, in one piece
  2 cups Sushi Rice (at right)

Dipping Sauce

  2 tablespoons wasabi (see note above)
  ¼ cup soy sauce
  2 tablespoons minced green onion
  1 tablespoon rice wine

1. In a small bowl mix wasabi with just enough cold water to form a thick paste. Set aside. In another bowl combine rice vinegar and water. Slice fish into 24 one-ounce portions.

2. Using the vinegar-water solution to keep your hands damp, pick up a small portion of rice and gently form it into a small oval. Dot the top of the oval with a little wasabi paste and place a slice of tuna on top. Repeat with remaining rice and tuna. Arrange sushi on a platter, preferably a Japanese-style lacquer or porcelain tray. Serve with Dipping Sauce.

Makes 2 dozen sushi.

Dipping Sauce Combine wasabi with just enough cold water to form a thick paste. Just before serving, combine wasabi paste, soy sauce, green onions, and rice wine.

SUSHI RICE

  3⅓ cups short-grain rice
  4 cups water
  1 three-inch square of konbu (dried kelp, available in Japanese markets; optional)

Dressing

  5 to 6 tablespoons rice vinegar
  5 tablespoons sugar
  4 teaspoons salt

1. Place rice in a large bowl; cover with cold water. Run hands through rice to remove starch, until water turns cloudy. Drain. Repeat until water remains clear. Drain again.

2. Place rice in saucepan with the water. Place konbu, if used, on top. Cover saucepan and bring to a boil over high heat; boil 2 minutes. Reduce heat to medium and boil, covered, for 5 minutes. Reduce heat to lowest possible setting and cook until all moisture is absorbed, about 15 minutes. Uncover; place a towel over the top of the pot, and cover again. Let rest 15 minutes.

3. Add Dressing to sushi rice and mix well. Sushi rice may be kept in a cool place, covered with a damp cloth, for up to 2 days; it should not be refrigerated.

Makes about 6 cups.

Dressing In a small saucepan over low heat, combine all ingredients and cook until sugar and salt dissolve. Cool to room temperature. Keeps indefinitely.

HOW TO MAKE SUSHI

Nigiri Sushi—ovals of vinegar-seasoned rice with other ingredients layered on top—offer novices a way to make sushi without having to buy special tools and equipment.

Use only the very freshest fish and shellfish for sushi. Tuna is one of the prettiest and tastiest fish to use for nigiri sushi; salmon also works well. Purchase a boned fillet and follow step 2 to slice it to best effect. Shrimp makes a particularly eye-catching nigiri sushi; step 3 shows how to butterfly it. You can also top the Sushi Rice with a single oyster (see photograph, step 6).

It's important that the Sushi Rice have the right consistency. Follow the recipe on the opposite page, cutting in the Dressing with a vertical motion as shown in step 1.

Serve your sushi soon after you have made them; they quickly lose the freshness that makes them so succulent.

1. *With a thin tool like a wooden spatula held vertically, cut rice-vinegar Dressing (see Sushi Rice recipe opposite) into cooked rice, being careful not to mash the rice. Mix until the rice is glossy and holds together but is not mushy.*

2. *Slice boned fish fillet across the grain, approximately ¼ inch thick, to fit the shape of the rice oval (see step 4).*

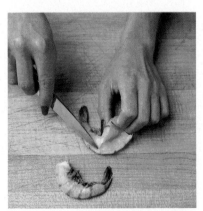

3. *To butterfly shrimp, using a sharp knife, slit the shrimp down its back, being careful not to cut all the way through. Gently flatten out the shrimp, with the cut side down.*

4. *Moisten hands with mixture of rice vinegar and water (see Nigiri Sushi recipe opposite). Form a small amount of Sushi Rice into an oval.*

5. *Finished Nigiri Sushi: Rice oval is topped with a dab of wasabi paste and a slice of fish or a butterflied shrimp.*

6. *A platter of Nigiri Sushi ready for presentation. From bottom: salmon, smoked eel, butterflied shrimp, and oyster, accompanied by a spoonful of wasabi paste and thin-sliced pickled ginger.*

Colorful sauces—from top, Salsa Verde, Homemade Cocktail Sauce, and Saffron Hollandaise— will enhance any shellfish platter or buffet. Offer a single sauce, or several, with steamed mussels, boiled shrimp, raw clams, grilled squid, or virtually any shellfish that's simply prepared.

SHELLFISH SAUCES: A BAKER'S HALF-DOZEN

Seven easy sauces to serve with shellfish—cold or hot—what more does a host or hostess need? Not much, except for a good seafood supplier. There simply is no more appetizing sight than a platter of seafood with sauces to match. Shrimp, crab, lobster, scallops, clams, mussels, oysters . . . These are always appropriate hors d'oeuvres, and while they're never inexpensive, they require no other adornment than a homemade dipping sauce.

Best-Ever Remoulade

    2 cups minced green onions
    ¾ cup Dijon mustard
    ½ cup mild sweet mustard
    1 tablespoon hot chili oil
    ⅓ cup prepared horseradish
    ⅓ cup catsup
    ¼ cup paprika
    ½ cup olive oil
    6 bay leaves

    2 tablespoons minced garlic
    3 cups minced celery
    1½ bunches parsley, finely minced
    2 lemons, peeled and all white
       pith removed, sectioned, seed-
       ed, and cut into ¼-inch dice
       Hot-pepper sauce, salt, and
       lemon juice to taste

1. Combine green onion, mustards, chili oil, horseradish, catsup, paprika, olive oil, bay leaves, and garlic in a food processor fitted with the steel blade, or a blender. Blend until smooth.

2. Transfer mixture to a bowl and stir in celery, parsley, and lemons. Season to taste with hot-pepper sauce, salt, and lemon juice. Taste again just before serving; adjust seasoning if necessary.

Makes about 8 cups.

Warm Parsley Sauce

Keep this sauce warm in a chafing dish and serve with chilled scallops, crab legs, or shrimp.

    4 cups parsley, leafy part only
    2 cups whipping cream
    2 shallots, minced
    ½ cup dry white wine
    ¼ cup cold butter, cut into
       4 pieces
       Salt and pepper

1. Blanch parsley in boiling water 20 seconds; drain and transfer to a bowl of ice water to stop the cooking and set the color. Drain and dry thoroughly on paper towels. Chop by hand or in a food processor until almost puréed.

2. In a medium saucepan over high heat, reduce cream by half. In a medium skillet over high heat, cook shallots and wine until wine has almost evaporated. Add the hot reduced cream and whisk well. Remove from heat and whisk in butter, one piece at a time, until it is all incorporated. Add minced parsley and salt and pepper to taste.

Makes 1¾ cups.

Sicilian Dipping Sauce

Balsamic vinegar is a very mild, almost sweet, wood-aged vinegar from Italy. It can be found in fine food markets and is worth every penny. Serve this cool, fresh sauce with skewers of hot grilled fish or oysters on the half-shell.

- 1½ cups tomatoes, peeled, seeded, and finely chopped
- ⅓ cup minced yellow onions
  Half a red bell pepper, minced
- 2 tablespoons balsamic vinegar
- ¼ cup olive oil
- ½ to ¾ teaspoon dried hot red pepper flakes
  Freshly ground black pepper and salt to taste

Combine tomatoes, onions, and red bell pepper in a bowl and set aside. In a small bowl whisk together vinegar, olive oil, hot pepper flakes, and black pepper. Pour over tomatoes and let marinate 30 minutes. Add salt to taste just before serving.

Makes 2 cups.

Homemade Cocktail Sauce

This sauce not only can be made ahead, it should be. It's far superior to the storebought variety and allows you to adjust seasonings to your taste.

- ¼ cup catsup
- ½ cup chili sauce
- 1 teaspoon chili powder
- 2 tablespoons lemon juice
- 2 to 3 tablespoons freshly grated horseradish or 2 tablespoons prepared horseradish
- 1 teaspoon minced garlic

At least 48 hours before serving, combine catsup, chili sauce, chili powder, lemon juice, horseradish, and garlic in a stainless steel, glass, or ceramic bowl. Cover and refrigerate until serving time. Bring to room temperature before serving. Cocktail sauce can be made up to 5 days ahead.

Makes 1 cup.

Saffron Hollandaise

Saffron complements almost all fish and shellfish. Here, it imparts its rich flavor and color to a satiny hollandaise, to spoon over hot steamed mussels or clams.

- 1 cup butter
- ¾ teaspoon saffron threads
- 6 egg yolks, at room temperature
- ¼ cup lemon juice
  Salt and cayenne pepper to taste

1. In a small pan over low heat, melt butter; add saffron. Remove from heat and set aside to cool slightly.

2. In top of a double boiler, combine egg yolks and lemon juice. Whisk well. Place over simmering water and whisk constantly until mixture begins to thicken. Add melted butter drop by drop, whisking constantly. Mixture should emulsify, becoming silky and shiny as egg yolks absorb butter. When all butter has been incorporated, season to taste with salt and cayenne. Serve immediately, or keep warm in a double boiler.

Makes 1½ cups.

Salsa Verde
Green tomato sauce

If you make this salsa several hours ahead—and there's no reason not to—don't add salt until just before serving. That way the tomatillos, onions, and green onions will stay crisp and firm. Salsa verde complements any seafood; it's particularly delicious with raw or grilled oysters.

- 1 pound tomatillos (Mexican green tomatoes, available in Hispanic markets), canned or fresh
- ¼ cup minced cilantro
- ½ cup diced white onion
- 2 to 3 serrano or jalapeño chiles, minced
- 2 green onions, minced
  Lemon juice to taste
  Salt to taste
  Additional minced cilantro, for garnish (optional)

1. Drain tomatillos if canned. If fresh, husk them and blanch them in boiling water to cover until tender, about 12 minutes; drain. Core tomatillos and mince.

2. In a small stainless steel, glass, or ceramic bowl combine tomatillos, cilantro, onion, chiles, green onion, and lemon juice to taste. Add salt to taste just before serving. *To make in a food processor*, put tomatillos, cilantro, onion, and chiles in work bowl fitted with steel blade; process briefly. Mixture should be slightly chunky. Stir in green onion by hand; add lemon juice and salt to taste just before serving.

Makes about 3 cups.

Tarragon and Anchovy Mayonnaise

Whisking by hand will produce the best texture for this lovely mayonnaise. Serve it with cold cracked crab or shrimp, or as a dip for deep-fried seafood: clams, oysters, shrimp, calamari, scallops, or strips of sole.

- 3 egg yolks
- 2 teaspoons lemon juice
- 1½ cups safflower oil
- ½ cup olive oil
- 1 dozen oil-packed anchovy fillets
- 1½ tablespoons fresh minced tarragon or 1 tablespoon dried
  Salt to taste

1. Combine egg yolks and lemon juice in a small bowl. Whisk together well. Begin adding safflower oil and olive oil drop by drop, whisking continuously, until mixture thickens and emulsifies. *To make in a blender or food processor*, blend together egg yolks and lemon juice. With motor running, add oils drop by drop until mixture thickens and emulsifies.

2. Pound anchovies and their oil to a paste. Stir into mayonnaise along with tarragon. Add salt to taste.

Makes 2 cups.

MEATS AND POULTRY

Served as a preface to dinner, the best hors d'oeuvres are modestly portioned and light. But at more and more cocktail parties, the hors d'oeuvre course *replaces* dinner; if that's the plan, the host or hostess should provide a hearty and generous selection, the better to cushion the cocktails and satisfy hunger.

Meat- and poultry-based hors d'oeuvres fill that bill nicely. You probably wouldn't want to serve them before a full-course lunch or dinner, but they are perfect for cocktail buffets or open houses, where guests will appreciate their appetite-appeasing power.

The hors d'oeuvres in this section are an international lot, covering ground from Japan and Thailand to Argentina. When making your menu, avoid mixing cuisines. A platter of Texas-Style Cocktail Ribs (see page 54) is most appealing in the presence of other southwestern foods: tortillas and salsa, tiny bean-filled burritos, miniature jalapeño cornbread squares, and the like. Any of the following substantial hors d'oeuvres can suggest a theme for the rest of the menu, thereby prompting ideas for everything from decor to drinks.

MATAMBRE

Matambre ("kill hunger") is an Argentine specialty, a delightfully handsome beef dish from a beef-eating country. A flank steak is butterflied and marinated, stuffed with brightly colored spinach, carrots, and eggs, then rolled, baked and sliced. The result is a spiral of vivid colors that tastes as good as it looks!

    2 pounds flank steak
    3 cloves garlic, finely minced
    ¾ cup red wine
    2 tablespoons soy sauce
    ½ teaspoon hot red pepper flakes
    2 tablespoons olive oil

    2 tablespoons butter
    ½ cup chopped onion
    2 medium carrots, peeled
    1 pound spinach leaves, cleaned
       and stemmed
    2 hard-boiled eggs, each sliced
       into 6 rounds

1. Have butcher butterfly flank steak, or butterfly it yourself by slicing horizontally along its longest side, almost but not quite all the way through. Open steak out flat and pound with a mallet to an even ¼-inch thickness.

2. Combine garlic, red wine, soy sauce, pepper flakes, and olive oil. Put meat in a stainless steel, glass, or ceramic bowl and pour marinade over it. Cover and let marinate 2 to 4 hours or overnight.

3. Preheat oven to 350° F. Heat butter in a small skillet. Add onion and sauté until soft, about 10 minutes. Set aside. Parboil whole carrots in boiling salted water about 3 minutes; drain. Remove meat from marinade and lay out flat. Arrange raw spinach leaves in a sheet on the surface of the meat; then arrange egg slices, carrots, and onions on top of the spinach. Roll up the flank steak and tie it with string at 3-inch intervals. Bake 1 hour.

4. Let matambre cool completely; refrigerate several hours for easier slicing. Slice roll into 12 thin slices.

Makes 1 dozen cocktail slices.

Make-Ahead Tip Matambre may be cooked up to 2 days in advance.

STUFFED BREAST OF VEAL, ROMAN STYLE

A whole boned breast of veal, laid flat, is perfect for stuffing. Wrap it around a savory herbed mixture of ground veal, pork, and spinach, then bake it in a foil or paper package. Cooled and thinly sliced, it makes a striking edible mosaic to serve with Chardonnay or a light Italian red wine. Make it part of an antipasto or a platter of cold

cuts, or serve it on its own with a basket of warm toasted Cocktail Crumpets (see page 79) or Cocktail Scones (see page 30).

    1 boned whole breast of veal
    ¾ pound ground veal
    ¼ pound ground pork
    ⅓ cup shelled pistachio nuts
    ½ cup freshly grated Parmesan
       cheese
    1 cup cooked chopped spinach
    ⅓ cup fresh soft bread crumbs
    3 shallots, minced
       Salt and black pepper to taste
    2 eggs, lightly beaten
    1 teaspoon dried oregano
    1 teaspoon dried thyme
    2 tablespoons olive oil
    2 tablespoons Madeira

1. Preheat oven to 350° F. Lay boned breast out flat. In a large bowl combine ground veal, ground pork, pistachios, Parmesan, spinach, bread crumbs, shallots, salt, pepper, eggs, oregano, and thyme. Mix lightly with your hands. Fry a little piece of the mixture and taste; adjust seasonings if necessary.

2. Arrange the stuffing in an even strip lengthwise down the center of the breast. Fold the sides of the breast up and over the stuffing, then use a trussing needle and strong thread to sew up the seam.

3. Combine olive oil and Madeira and brush the mixture on a piece of parchment paper or aluminum foil large enough to encase the stuffed veal breast. Set the breast in the center of the oiled paper or foil, bring the ends of the paper or foil up and seal. Twist the ends shut.

4. Bake 1½ hours. Let rest a few minutes before slicing. Serve hot, warm, or cool, but not chilled, in very thin slices.

Makes 18 to 20 cocktail slices.

Neatly sliced Matambre, a roll of marinated beef stuffed with eggs and vegetables, makes a festive and unusual buffet dish.

Meaty Texas-Style Cocktail Ribs can be baked, broiled, or grilled. The secret is in the sauce—a lip-smacking, power-packing, fingerlicking-good one from Big D.

TEXAS-STYLE COCKTAIL RIBS

Here's a wicked "cue" from some Dallas folks who know a thing or two about barbecued ribs. Set out tortilla chips and salsa, with plenty of napkins and beer. These sweet and tangy riblets are irresistible.

> 8 pounds country-style pork ribs, cut into small riblets by your butcher

Sauce

> 3 cloves garlic, chopped
> 2 small hot dried red chiles
> 1 tablespoon chopped cilantro (optional)
> 1 teaspoon ground cumin
> 1 teaspoon salt
> ¼ cup brown sugar
> 2 tablespoons Worcestershire sauce
> 2 cups chili sauce
> 2 cups tomato catsup
> 2 cups white vinegar
> Few drops hot-pepper sauce

1. Preheat oven to 325° F. *To prepare the sauce:* Combine garlic, chiles, cilantro (if used), cumin, salt, sugar, and Worcestershire sauce in a blender. Blend well.

2. In a saucepan, combine garlic mixture, chili sauce, catsup, vinegar and hot-pepper sauce. Simmer 25 minutes, uncovered. Sauce will be thick and will thicken even more as it cools.

3. Place riblets in a large roasting pan. Pour sauce evenly over the ribs. Cover and bake 2 hours.

4. Preheat broiler or prepare a charcoal fire. Grill ribs for 6 to 8 minutes or broil for 3 to 4 minutes, turning them once and basting with sauce until they are browned and crusty. Charcoal grilling gives the most authentic flavor.

Makes about 25 ribs.

Make-Ahead Tip Sauce can be made up to 1 week in advance and stored in the refrigerator. Ribs can be baked several hours in advance and grilled or broiled just before serving.

STUFFED CHICKEN BREASTS WITH MANY MUSHROOMS

Slice these stuffed and rolled breasts to reveal eye-catching spirals of light and dark: ivory chicken wrapped around a dusky Oriental filling of green onions, ginger, and dried black mushrooms. A rice flour coating seals in juices when the rolls are deep-fried and adds a crisp, golden crust.

> 3 to 4 dried shiitake mushrooms or Chinese black mushrooms, about 1½ inches in diameter
> ½ pound white button mushrooms, cleaned and minced
> 2 green onions, minced
> 1 carrot, peeled and minced
> Salt and black pepper to taste
> 1 tablespoon butter
> 2 tablespoons vegetable oil
> 2 shallots, minced
> 1 tablespoon minced ginger
> 2 teaspoons minced garlic

1 tablespoon sake
1 teaspoon sesame oil
2 eggs, separated
2 whole chicken breasts,
skinned, boned, and halved
Rice flour or cornstarch
Approximately 6 cups corn oil
for deep-frying

1. Soak dried mushrooms in warm water for 30 minutes. Squeeze them dry, cut off the tough stems, and mince the caps. In a bowl combine minced black and white mushrooms, green onion, and carrot. Season well with salt and pepper.

2. In a large skillet melt butter with oil over moderate heat. Add shallots and cook until soft but not browned, about 10 minutes. Add ginger and garlic and cook 2 to 3 minutes longer. Add mushroom mixture and sake. Simmer 10 to 15 minutes or until mixture is quite dry. Mushrooms will exude a lot of water while cooking but will gradually cook dry. Add sesame oil and lightly beaten egg yolks and set aside.

3. Pound chicken-breast halves into neat rectangles, approximately 2½ inches by 3½ inches. Sprinkle lightly on both sides with rice flour. Spread 2 tablespoons filling on each breast. Roll up and tie with string.

4. Dip each breast in lightly beaten egg white, then in rice flour or cornstarch. Heat corn oil to 375° F. Deep-fry rolls until crisp and golden, about 5 to 6 minutes. Drain on paper towels and let cool slightly. Cut rolls on the diagonal into 6 slices each. Serve hot.

Makes about 2 dozen slices.

Make-Ahead Tip Chicken breasts can be stuffed and dipped in egg white and rice flour up to 1 hour ahead. Set coated rolls on a cookie sheet; refrigerate until ready to fry.

CAILLETTES

What the French call *caillettes* ("little quail") are actually well-seasoned rounds of ground pork, rice, and spinach. Lacy caul fat (from around the intestine, usually pork) makes the prettiest wrapper for these little pork balls, but thin-sliced bacon is a good runner-up. You can also pack this mixture into a bacon-lined loaf pan or terrine and make a perfectly splendid meat loaf; bake it until the juices run clear, and serve with a fresh tomato sauce.

2 pounds chicken livers
Salt and black pepper to taste
2 tablespoons flour
2 tablespoons olive oil
2 shallots, finely minced
2 pounds lean ground pork
1 cup cooked white rice
1 pound fresh spinach, washed, stemmed, and chopped
½ cup minced parsley
2 cloves garlic, minced (optional)
1½ teaspoons minced fresh thyme or 1 teaspoon dried
3 eggs, lightly beaten
1 pound caul fat (available at some butcher shops) or thin-sliced bacon

1. Preheat oven to 425° F. Trim livers of any fat or tough spots, chop them coarsely, and put in a bowl. Sprinkle with salt and pepper to taste and flour.

2. In a large skillet over medium heat, heat olive oil. Add shallots and sauté until they are softened but not browned, about 10 minutes. Add livers and sauté over medium high heat 3 to 4 minutes, or until they are barely browned outside but still pink within.

3. Transfer livers to a bowl, leaving shallots in the skillet. Add pork to skillet and sauté 5 minutes, or until pork loses its raw red color but is not fully cooked.

4. Mix together livers, shallots, pork, rice, spinach, parsley, garlic (if used), thyme, and eggs. Shape into 1½-inch balls. Wrap each ball in a small square of caul fat or thin strip of bacon. Place on a cookie sheet and bake until crisp and golden brown (20 to 25 minutes).

Makes about 100 small caillettes.

APPLEWOOD-SMOKED BEEF

Delicious smoked meats are well within the province of any home cook with a barbecue grill. Here, applewood chips (you'll need about 5 pounds) lend their distinctive fragrance to a whole cross-rib roast via a technique that could hardly be easier. Slice the roast thinly and serve it in miniature open-faced sandwiches made of a good rye bread, homemade mayonnaise or horseradish sauce, and paper-thin onion rings on top.

1 cross-rib roast, approximately 8 pounds, boned and tied
Salt and black pepper to taste

Season meat with salt and pepper. Build a large charcoal fire, preferably with mesquite charcoal. Soak 5 pounds applewood chips in water for 15 to 20 minutes. When the coals are completely white (about 40 minutes), spread soaked chips over them evenly. Put beef on grill rack, fat side down, cover, and roast approximately 3 hours. Check internal temperature of meat with a meat thermometer. If the roast is not sufficiently cooked to your liking, complete the roasting in a preheated 350° F oven to avoid smoking the meat any further. Let rest at least 10 minutes before slicing, or let cool completely and chill before slicing.

Makes approximately 50 thin slices.

PETER TAMANO'S TWICE-FRIED WINGS

Who ever heard of a batter-fried dish that could be made ahead and re-heated? That's the beauty of this recipe from San Francisco chef Peter Tamano. His technique yields a juicy fried chicken wing in a light, well-seasoned coating. Be careful not to overmix the batter or your coating will be tough. Wings can be fried in large batches the second time around; they will not stick together.

> 5 green onions, trimmed and flattened with the side of a knife
> 5 quarter-sized slices fresh ginger, flattened with the side of a knife
> 4 cups water
> 1¾ cups flour
> 1 teaspoon salt
> 2 tablespoons peanut oil
> ¼ cup sweet rice wine (mirin)
> 2 tablespoons soy sauce
> 25 chicken wings
> Peanut oil for deep-frying
> Choice of Dipping Sauce (see pages 37–39)

1. Put green onions, ginger, and water in a bowl and set aside for 25 minutes. Strain water and discard green onion and ginger.

2. Add flour, salt, oil, rice wine, and soy sauce to the flavored water. Combine gently with a fork; batter should be lumpy and fairly thin. Dip the chicken wings in the batter and set on a towel or cookie sheet.

3. Heat plenty of oil in a large pot, a deep fryer, or a wok until oil reaches 375° F. Cook wings, 4 or 5 at a time, just until edges begin to color. Remove to a paper towel. Skim oil periodically to remove any pieces of cooked batter. When all wings have been fried once, refry them until they are quite crisp and brown, being sure to maintain oil at a constant 375° F. Drain on paper towels and serve immediately with sauce.

Makes 25 wings.

Make-Ahead Tip Surprisingly enough, the wings can be fried once, then covered and refrigerated for up to 1 week. Refry just before serving.

POLLO PEQUEÑO

Many supermarkets are now selling what look like tiny chicken "legs," called "drummettes." You can simply use chicken wings with the wing tips removed—not so fancy, but just as delicious. After a bath in a spicy, sweet-and-tangy marinade—overnight, if possible—the chicken can be cooked in any of three ways: baking, broiling, or grilling. Baking instructions are given below; broiling takes about 5 to 6 minutes. Perhaps the tastiest results come from the charcoal grill, where the chicken can be cooked and basted for 12 to 15 minutes, until it is crisp and richly browned.

> 24 chicken "drummettes" or wings
> ½ cup dry sherry
> 2 tablespoons sherry vinegar
> 2 tablespoons lemon juice
> 1 tablespoon tomato paste
> 1 tablespoon sugar
> 2 tablespoons minced garlic
> 2 teaspoons salt
> 2 tablespoons ground cumin
> ½ teaspoon cayenne pepper
> 2 tablespoons chopped cilantro, for garnish

1. If you are using chicken wings, cut off wing tips. In a stainless steel, glass, or ceramic bowl, combine sherry, vinegar, lemon juice, tomato paste, sugar, garlic, salt, cumin, and cayenne. Marinate chicken in mixture for at least 4 hours or overnight.

2. Preheat oven to 350° F. Bake chicken uncovered for 45 minutes. Serve hot, garnished with chopped cilantro.

Makes 2 dozen.

CARNITAS

A favorite snack in Mexico, *carnitas* ("little meats") are made from thin strips of pork cooked slowly un-til tender and crisp. There's no point in using an expensive cut for this dish; the best carnitas are made from pork well marbled with fat. Wrapped in a warm tortilla with a piquant salsa and sour cream, they make a thoroughly beguiling addition to a south-of-the-border menu.

> 30 small, fresh corn or flour tortillas
> 5 pounds boneless pork shoulder
> 2 teaspoons salt
> Salsa Verde (see page 51)
> Sour cream

1. If desired, use a 4-inch biscuit cutter to cut smaller rounds from the tortillas. The 4-inch rounds are easier to maneuver as finger food.

2. Cut meat into thin rectangles, approximately 2 inches by 4 inches by ¼ thick. Sprinkle meat with salt and put into a large, shallow pot with just enough water to cover. Bring to a boil slowly, then adjust heat to maintain a steady simmer. Cook until water evaporates and meat is very tender, about 1 to 1¼ hours.

3. Continue cooking meat slowly in its own rendered fat for 20 to 25 minutes, or until strips are quite crisp. Serve hot, tucked into tortillas with spoonfuls of salsa and sour cream.

Makes about 30.

SCOTCH CHICKEN

Golden Scotch whiskey adds its suave and mellow flavor to the cream sauce binding this dish. If all the ingre-dients are ready, the sautéing and saucing of the chicken is just a matter of minutes.

> 1 cup plus 3 tablespoons Scotch whiskey
> 1½ cups raisins
> 1½ pounds skinned and boned chicken breasts
> ¼ cup flour

Salt
¾ cup butter
3 shallots, minced
⅓ cup whipping cream
⅓ cup chicken stock
    Minced parsley, for garnish

1. Heat 1 cup of the whiskey in a small saucepan until warm. Add raisins, cover and remove from heat. Let steep ½ hour.

2. Cut chicken into 1½-inch cubes. Dust with flour and sprinkle lightly with salt. Melt half the butter in a large heavy skillet over moderately high heat and sauté chicken, in batches if necessary to prevent crowding, 2 to 3 minutes or until just cooked through. Transfer to a platter and keep warm in oven.

3. Add remaining butter to saucepan and sauté shallots until soft but not browned. Add raisins and their Scotch marinade. Simmer 5 minutes. Warm remaining 3 tablespoons Scotch in a small saucepan. Add to raisins and ignite with a match. When flames die down, add cream and stock. Simmer 3 minutes.

4. Return chicken cubes to sauce and stir to coat. Serve at once on cocktail picks, taking care to spear a few raisins along with the chicken. Garnish with minced parsley.

Makes 2 dozen cocktail bites.

GRILLED CHICKEN LIVERS WITH SHERRY-VINEGAR CREAM

Skewered livers napped with a reduction of butter, cream, and sherry vinegar make a succulent hot nibble with sherry or cocktails. Use only fresh livers; select pale ones if possible. If you are using wooden skewers, soak them in water for several hours to prevent their burning.

1 pound pale, fresh chicken
    or duck livers
½ cup milk
½ cup unsalted butter

2 tablespoons sherry vinegar or
    fruit vinegar
2 tablespoons whipping cream
    Salt and freshly ground black
    pepper

1. Preheat broiler or prepare a charcoal fire. Trim all fat and tough spots from livers. Soak in milk for 30 minutes. Thread on 24 small skewers.

2. Melt butter in a large skillet over moderately high heat until it begins to brown. Add vinegar and remove from heat. Brush livers with butter mixture, then broil or grill, basting once or twice, until livers are browned outside but still pink within.

3. In a small saucepan, combine remaining butter mixture and cream. Cook until slightly thickened. Add salt and pepper to taste. Arrange skewers on a warm serving platter, spoon the sauce over, and serve hot.

Makes about 2 dozen small skewers.

Plump chicken wings marinated in a spicy, tomato-based sauce turn crisp and brown on the charcoal grill. Pollo Pequeño is a multi-napkin nibble, casual fare for a summer picnic or Latin fiesta.

TERIYAKI CHICKEN

A soy-based marinade does double duty for this dish. Half of it is used to marinate the chicken overnight; the other half is reduced to a suave Oriental glaze for the finished chicken. Serve them hot with cocktail picks, or arrange them in small lettuce "cups" for guests to pick up and fold themselves—an eye-opening contrast of hot, cool, and crunchy.

    2 whole chicken breasts, skinned
       and boned
       Salt
    2 tablespoons minced fresh
       ginger
    ¼ cup soy sauce
    ¼ cup sweet rice wine (mirin) or
       slightly sweet Sauterne-type
       cooking wine
    2 tablespoons sesame oil
    2 tablespoons finely minced
       garlic
       Vegetable oil for sautéing
       Grated rind of 1 lemon
    ¼ cup finely minced green onion

1. Cut each breast in half, then cut each half into 5 cubes. Sprinkle chicken lightly with salt.

2. In a medium stainless steel, glass, or ceramic bowl, combine ginger, soy sauce, rice wine, sesame oil, and garlic. Set aside half the marinade. Pour remaining marinade over chicken, cover, and let marinate overnight.

3. Heat a thin film of vegetable oil in a large, heavy skillet over high heat. When oil is almost smoking, add chicken pieces and cook rapidly for 15 seconds. Add reserved marinade and bring to a boil.

4. Remove chicken pieces to a serving platter. Add lemon rind and green onion to the pan. Cook over high heat until sauce is reduced to about 2 tablespoons. Spoon sauce over chicken and serve immediately with cocktail picks.

Makes 20 cocktail "bites."

GREEN ONIONS IN SILKY BEEF

These beef-wrapped green-onion rolls are featured at most Japanese *robata* restaurants—restaurants that specialize in simple charcoal grilling— where a *robata* chef will grill them to order over hot coals. A soy-based marinade tenderizes and flavors the beef; the green-onion center adds a pungent accent. Serve the sliced rolls on a Japanese-style black lacquered tray for a particularly striking effect.

    1 pound very lean beef
    2 dozen green onions
    ¼ cup soy sauce
    ¼ cup sugar
    ¼ cup peanut or corn oil
    2 tablespoons rice wine
    2 tablespoons water
    1 tablespoon sesame seed

1. Slice beef into thin strips about 5 inches long and 1½ inches wide. You should have about 18 strips.

2. Trim and clean the green onions. Cut 18 green onions into 4-inch lengths, discarding the dark green tops. Slice the remaining green onions into thin rings; reserve for garnish.

3. Lay one 4-inch length of green onion in the center of each strip of meat, parallel to the 5-inch side. Roll meat around onion and secure with a toothpick. In a stainless steel, glass, or ceramic bowl, combine soy sauce, sugar, 2 tablespoons of the oil, the wine, and water. Pour marinade over green-onion rolls; cover and let marinate at least 1 hour at room temperature or refrigerate overnight.

4. Bring rolls to room temperature if necessary. Drain, reserving marinade. In a heavy skillet, heat remaining oil over high heat. Add green-onion rolls and brown quickly all over, in stages if necessary to prevent crowding. Add the reserved marinade and continue cooking rapidly about 3 minutes.

5. Remove rolls to a cutting board and cut each one in half. Arrange on a serving platter and serve hot, garnished with chopped green onions and sesame seed.

Makes about 3 dozen small rolls.

PORK IN GREEN CHILE

Cubes of pork cooked until tender in a highly seasoned sauce can be served on small skewers or wrapped in soft flour tortillas. Add a batch of margaritas and some spicy salsa music for a festive Latin touch to your cocktail party.

    2½ pounds boneless pork
        shoulder, cut into ½-inch
        cubes
     1 tablespoon salt
     4 cups water
     2 tablespoons minced garlic
     ¼ teaspoon ground cumin
     ½ teaspoon dried oregano
     2 to 3 fresh green chiles, seeded
     3 tablespoons peanut oil
     3 teaspoons flour
    36 small flour tortillas, cut into
        smaller rounds with a 4-inch
        biscuit cutter (optional)

1. In a large pot combine meat, salt, and water and bring to a boil. Reduce heat and simmer, covered, for 45 minutes. Uncover and continue cooking for 15 minutes, or until meat is tender and most of the liquid has evaporated.

2. Put garlic, cumin, oregano, and chiles in a blender. Blend well.

3. In a large skillet, brown meat in 3 batches, using 1 tablespoon oil per batch and dusting each batch with 1 teaspoon flour. Fry each batch until well browned and crisp, then transfer to a plate while you brown remaining pork. When all the pork has been browned, return all of it to the pot, add garlic-spice mixture, and simmer, stirring occasionally, for 15 minutes. Spear pork cubes with cocktail picks or small (6- to 8-inch) skewers and serve on a colorful plat-ter with remaining sauce drizzled over the top, or serve pork in a bowl with a napkin-lined basket of warm tortillas on the side.

Makes about 3 dozen cocktail skewers.

STILL LIFE OF COLD CUTS

An appetizer platter of cold cuts is common to many cuisines. To make a tempting arrangement at home, all you need is a good local deli and an eye for presentation.

Figure about 1½ ounces of cold cuts, sliced very thin, per person. Select a variety of meats, such as smoked turkey, prosciutto, and Westphalian ham. Add some cheeses, allowing an ounce per person of "slicing" cheeses like Jarlsberg and ¾ to 1 ounce per person of spread-able cheeses like Brie.

Olives, pickles, or chutneys, and of course good bread or crackers, should round out the cold cut platter. Pro-vide small forks for the various meats and sliced cheeses, and a separate knife for each spreadable cheese.

Cold cuts are always a welcome addition to a spread of hors d'oeuvres. Choose whatever looks good at the local delicatessen and add an assortment of cheeses, plain crackers, good bread, and a relish or pickle to complete the appetizing equation.

Peppery Thai Pork Balls are rolled in rice noodles and fried to produce a moist meatball with a crisp coating. They are made with nam pla, a pungent sauce that distinguishes dozens of Thai dishes and dipping sauces.

THE INTERNATIONAL MEATBALL

Chafing dish meatballs can draw a yawn from the most well-bred party-goer. Swedish meatballs *again?* It's time to put that classic out to pasture and explore some other ways with the ubiquitous meatball. The methods are different and the seasonings change, but the meatball in one form or another is a respected part of almost every national cuisine.

A good, well-seasoned meatball makes outstanding cocktail fare—a savory mouthful that guests can spear cleanly with a pick. A handsome set of reusable picks is a good investment; for large parties, select some attractive disposable ones.

Most meatball mixtures can be made and shaped in advance, then broiled or grilled at the last moment. The selection that follows is a quick cook's tour of a few of the most intriguing international renditions.

THAI PORK BALLS WITH CRUNCHY NOODLES

The meatballs below are infused with *nam pla,* a pungent fermented fish sauce, then coated with rice noodles and deep-fried until crunchy. A chile-laden dipping sauce adds the fiery finishing touch.

- 1 pound lean ground pork
- 1 tablespoon minced garlic
- 1 tablespoon freshly ground black pepper
- 1 teaspoon salt
- ¼ cup nam pla
- 3 to 4 ounces rice stick noodles (available in Oriental markets)
- 2 eggs, lightly beaten
  Peanut oil for deep-frying

Sweet and Fiery Dipping Sauce

- 2 cups white vinegar
- 2 cups sugar
- 1 tablespoon salt
- 6 cloves garlic, minced
- 8 small, fresh red chiles, finely sliced

1. In a bowl mix together pork, garlic, pepper, salt, and nam pla. Shape into 16 small balls.

2. Cook noodles 1½ minutes in plenty of boiling salted water; drain and rinse under cold water.

3. Dip each pork ball into beaten eggs, then wrap in boiled rice noodles, pressing firmly to make noodles adhere. Heat oil in a deep skillet or wok to 375° F. Fry balls a few at a time until they are crisp and browned. Drain briefly on paper towels, then serve hot with Sweet and Fiery Dipping Sauce.

Makes 1 dozen cocktail meatballs.

Sweet and Fiery Dipping Sauce

Put vinegar, sugar, salt, garlic, and chiles in a saucepan. Bring to a boil, stirring. Remove from heat and let cool. Serve at room temperature. For a slightly milder version, strain out chiles after boiling.

Make-Ahead Tip Pork mixture may be combined one day in advance; coat with noodles just before frying. Dipping sauce may be made 2 days in advance.

PORK BALLS IN HOISIN SAUCE

Hoisin sauce, available in Chinese markets, adds a sweetness to these meatballs. They are as fun to eat as they are to make, served in cool lettuce "cups" with a dab of hoisin sauce and a shower of green onion and chopped toasted peanuts.

> 2 pounds ground pork butt
> 2 tablespoons each *finely minced garlic and minced fresh ginger*
> ⅓ cup hoisin sauce
> ⅓ cup soy sauce
> ¼ cup sugar
> ¼ cup rice wine (mirin)
> ¼ cup minced water chestnuts
> ¼ cup minced shrimp
> 1 egg white
>   Approximately 2 cups chicken stock

> Lettuce leaves, hoisin sauce, chopped green onions, and chopped toasted peanuts for garnish

1. Combine pork, garlic, ginger, hoisin sauce, soy sauce, sugar, rice wine, water chestnuts, shrimp, and egg white. Cover; refrigerate overnight.

2. Form pork mixture into 24 small balls. Bring chicken stock just to a simmer in a large saucepan and add pork balls. Stock should just barely cover pork balls; add more stock during cooking if necessary. Pan should not be crowded; cook pork balls in two batches if necessary. Simmer, covered, for 15 to 20 minutes. Serve hot.

Makes 2 dozen small pork balls.

Make-Ahead Tip Pork balls may be cooked in stock several hours ahead; rewarm in a 300° F oven.

BLACK PEPPERCORN MEATBALLS WITH ANCHOVY SAUCE

Steak *au poivre* in meatball form is bound to please the beef eaters. These pepper-coated meatballs can be broiled or grilled and basted with anchovy sauce, as described below, or they can be pan-fried in the anchovy-butter mixture and served in a chafing dish with their sauce.

> 2 pounds ground sirloin
> 1 tablespoon olive oil
> 2 tablespoons black peppercorns
> ½ cup butter, melted
> 3 anchovy fillets, minced
> 1 clove garlic, minced
> 2 tablespoons Cognac or other brandy

1. Preheat broiler or prepare a charcoal fire. Mix meat and olive oil together lightly. Form into 24 small balls. Lightly crush peppercorns in a pepper grinder or with the back of a heavy skillet. Roll balls in the crushed pepper.

2. In a small skillet, heat butter and anchovies, mashing anchovies against the side of the skillet with a wooden spoon until they are pasty. Add garlic and sauté slowly 3 minutes. Add Cognac and ignite.

3. Baste meatballs with anchovy sauce, then broil or grill until browned outside but still pink within, basting once or twice with more sauce. Serve meatballs with cocktail picks and put remaining sauce in a ramekin alongside.

Makes 2 dozen cocktail meatballs.

SPICY PERSIAN LAMB BALLS

Exotically spiced ground lamb surrounds a hidden whole almond to make a meatball that's more than a little out of the ordinary. Serve these with cocktail picks and a bowl of spicy Curry Sauce (see page 39), or with a dipping sauce of yogurt mixed with garlic, salt, and pepper. You might add a basket of warm pita bread triangles so guests can make their own "sandwiches."

> 2½ pounds lean ground lamb
> ⅓ cup chopped cilantro
> 1 teaspoon ground cumin
> ½ teaspoon ground cinnamon
> ⅛ teaspoon ground cloves
> 2 tablespoons finely minced ginger
> 1 teaspoon dry mustard
> 2 tablespoons lemon juice
>   Salt and black pepper to taste
> 36 whole toasted almonds

1. Preheat broiler or prepare a charcoal grill. In a large bowl combine lamb, cilantro, cumin, cinnamon, cloves, ginger, mustard, lemon juice, and salt and pepper to taste. Mix lightly but well. Shape seasoned lamb into a ball around one whole almond, covering the nut completely. Refrigerate 30 minutes or freeze 10 minutes.

2. Broil or grill meatballs until browned and crisp. Serve hot.

Makes 3 dozen small meatballs.

A TRIO OF KEBABS

Good cooking doesn't get much easier than the grilling of skewered foods. The most ancient and the most straightforward form of cooking is also inarguably one of the best—especially for cocktail fare.

Skewered foods are managed easily by guests; they can be assembled several hours ahead, then broiled or grilled at the last minute; and at an informal backyard party, they add an appetizing sight and smell, cooking away on the charcoal grill.

Any meat, intriguingly spiced or marinated, can be threaded on bamboo skewers and broiled or grilled. Keep pieces the same size for even cooking, and make sure that anything else you add to the skewers will cook in the same length of time. It's a good idea to soak wooden skewers in water several hours to prevent their burning.

The three recipes that follow span the globe—a good indication of just how versatile skewered fare can be.

SICILIAN PORK SKEWERS WITH SAGE

Pieces of prosciutto-wrapped pork, bread cubes, and sage are threaded on skewers and grilled to fragrant perfection, then basted with glistening anchovy butter.

- ½ pound prosciutto, sliced paper-thin and cut into 2-inch squares
- 2 pounds pork tenderloin, cut in ½-inch cubes
- 48 half-inch cubes of day-old French or Italian bread
- 24 fresh sage leaves (see Note) Olive oil

Anchovy Butter

- 1 cup unsalted butter
- 3 ounces anchovy fillets, drained and minced Lemon juice to taste

1. Wrap prosciutto around pork cubes. Using 6- to 8-inch bamboo skewers, thread each skewer with a bread cube, a cube of pork, a sage leaf, and a second bread cube. Drizzle olive oil over all and refrigerate overnight.

2. Preheat broiler or prepare a charcoal fire. Broil or grill skewers 9 to 12 minutes, basting with Anchovy Butter every 2 to 3 minutes. When pork is fully cooked but not dry, brush once again with Anchovy Butter and serve immediately.

Makes 2 dozen cocktail skewers.

Anchovy Butter In a large skillet, melt butter. Add anchovies; mash to a paste with the back of a wooden spoon. Add lemon juice to taste.

<u>Note</u> Dried bay leaves can be substituted for the sage.

BEEF SKEWERS, TAPAS STYLE

Tapas are the little hors d'oeuvres served in Spanish bars along with the sherry, often at no charge. This Spanish beef stew, its components threaded on skewers, becomes a marvelous tapa, to enjoy with a glass of dry sherry or a Spanish red wine.

- 3½ pounds beef tenderloin, cut into 2-ounce cubes
- 24 pitted prunes
- 24 large black Greek olives, unpitted
- ½ cup beef stock
- 2 tablespoons olive oil
- 3 tablespoons red wine
- 1 tablespoon tomato paste
- 2 tablespoons finely minced parsley mixed with 1 teaspoon grated orange rind

Marinade

- ⅓ cup red wine vinegar
- ¼ cup red wine
- ½ cup olive oil
- 2 tablespoons minced garlic Pinch powdered saffron
- 3 tablespoons minced fresh oregano or 1½ teaspoons dried
- 1 tablespoon chili powder
- ¼ cup brown sugar
- ¼ cup minced green onion

1. Put beef cubes, prunes, and olives into bowl with marinade; cover and marinate overnight.

2. Drain off and discard marinade. Reserve prunes. Put meat, olives, beef stock, olive oil, wine, and tomato paste into a large pot, bring to a simmer, and cook 1 hour, or until fork-tender. Lift meat and olives from sauce and let cool. Reserve sauce. Using 6- to 8-inch bamboo skewers, thread each skewer with a cube of beef, a prune, and an olive.

3. Preheat broiler. Broil skewers until meat is slightly crisp, about 5 minutes, turning once and basting with the reserved sauce. Serve garnished with parsley and orange rind.

Makes 2 dozen cocktail skewers.

Marinade Combine ingredients in a stainless steel, glass, or ceramic bowl.

INDONESIAN CHICKEN SKEWERS

Strips of chicken marinated in a sweet and peppery peanut sauce are threaded on skewers with red peppers and grilled until crisp and juicy.

- 3 whole chicken breasts, boned, skinned, and halved
- 1 cup crunchy peanut butter
- ⅓ cup chopped cilantro
- ½ cup chili sauce
- 1 tablespoon salt
- ½ teaspoon cayenne pepper
- ½ teaspoon black pepper
- ¼ cup lemon juice
- ¼ cup brown sugar
- ½ cup soy sauce
- 8 green onions, minced
- 3 tablespoons minced garlic
- 2 sweet bell peppers, red or green, cut into ½-inch cubes
  Minced parsley, for garnish

1. Slice each half-breast into four lengthwise strips. Set aside.

2. In a stainless steel, glass, or ceramic bowl, combine peanut butter, cilantro, chili sauce, salt, cayenne, black pepper, lemon juice, sugar, soy sauce, green onion, and garlic. Add chicken strips, cover, and let marinate overnight or up to 2 days.

3. Preheat broiler or prepare a charcoal fire. On 6- to 8-inch bamboo skewers, thread chicken strips like serpents, with pepper cubes interspersed. Broil or grill for 5 to 6 minutes, turning once. Serve garnished with minced parsley.

Makes 2 dozen cocktail kebabs.

Hot-off-the-grill Indonesian Chicken Skewers are an intriguing blend of sweet and spicy. Snaked around cubes of sweet peppers are strips of chicken infused with a lively peanut sauce.

FRUITS

Most hosts bring out the fruit at the *end* of the dinner, but some fruits do well in a savory setting, too. The cool freshness of sweet fruit can be remarkably appetizing, especially when combined with a salty element. A light-bodied Riesling or Chenin Blanc, perhaps with just a touch of sweetness, complements most hors d'oeuvres that have a fruit component.

MELON . . . OR PAPAYAS . . . OR PEARS . . . OR MANGO WITH PROSCIUTTO

Prosciutto-and-melon may be commonplace in Italian restaurants, but that doesn't mean it's dull. All that's required is paper-thin prosciutto and the sweetest, most fragrant melons you can find. The combination of salty ham with sweet, cold fruit is unforgettable. For a change of pace, or if the melons are not at their best, substitute papayas, pears, apples, or mango—or serve them all, complemented by a crisp, cold white wine.

> 1 large ripe, sweet melon of any variety, or 2 ripe papayas, pears, or mangoes, or any combination of these fruits
> Half a lemon
> 6 ounces prosciutto, sliced paper-thin
> Freshly ground black pepper
> Olive oil (optional)
> 1 tablespoon minced parsley

1. If using melon, cut away rind, then cut in half lengthwise. Scoop out seeds, then cut each half in half horizontally. Slice each quarter-melon into pieces about ½ inch wide. If using papayas, pears, or mangoes, peel the fruit, remove core or seeds, and slice into spears about ½ inch wide. Rub pears lightly with the lemon to prevent browning.

2. Wrap fruit in prosciutto slices, allowing ends of the fruit to poke out. Arrange fruit on a serving platter. Dust with pepper and drizzle lightly with olive oil (if used). Garnish with parsley.

Serves 12.

STEAMED FIGS CHINOISE

Marinate dried golden figs overnight to soften and flavor them, then stuff them with a gingery almond filling. Plumped over steaming rice wine, they make an unusual appetizer, to serve alone or to partner a platter of sliced ham or smoked duck. If you don't care for the pungent flavor of star anise, leave it out.

> 24 dried Calimyrna figs
> 1 cup rice wine
> 1 whole star anise (optional)
> 1 tablespoon peanut oil
> 1 teaspoon minced garlic
> 1 teaspoon minced ginger
> ¼ cup ground almonds
> ½ cup water

Tamari Almonds

> 24 whole almonds, unblanched
> 1 tablespoon peanut oil
> 1 tablespoon dark soy sauce or tamari (fermented soybean product, available in many health food stores and Oriental markets)
> Kosher salt

1. Soak figs overnight in ½ cup rice wine with the star anise (if used). When figs are plump and soft, cut off stem ends and hollow out a small space inside each. You may have to scoop out some of the fig pulp.

2. In a small skillet, heat oil over moderate heat. Add garlic and ginger and sauté 30 seconds. Add ground almonds and stir to blend. Remove from heat. Divide ground almond mixture among plumped figs, spooning it loosely into hollows. Set figs in a bamboo or metal steamer.

3. In bottom half of steamer, combine remaining ½ cup rice wine with the water. Bring to a boil, position

the top half of the steamer (with the figs) over the bottom half, cover, and steam until figs are hot, about 10 minutes. Garnish the top of each fig with a Tamari Almond and serve immediately.

Makes 2 dozen figs.

Tamari Almonds Tamari-roasted almonds are available in many health food stores. To make your own, preheat oven to 350° F. In a small bowl combine almonds, oil, and soy sauce. Toss well to coat almonds. Place almonds on a baking sheet, sprinkle with salt, and bake until dark brown and fragrant. When almonds are cool, they can be stored in an airtight container for up to a month.

PEPPERED PEARS

Served with a platter of sliced cold meats, especially ham, or as a piquant "aside" to pâtés, these pears are exquisite. Serve them with Quick Country Pâté (see page 24) or Duck Liver Pâté (see page 27) or with slices of Applewood-Smoked Beef (see page 55).

> 4 Bosc or other firm pears, peeled, halved, and cored
> 2 teaspoons coarsely ground black pepper
> Sugar
> ¼ cup dry white wine
> 1½ tablespoons unsalted butter

Preheat oven to 350° F. Place pear halves cut side down in an ovenproof baking dish. Sprinkle with pepper and dust lightly with sugar. Pour wine over pears; dot pears with butter. Cover and bake until pears are fork-tender, 30 to 45 minutes, uncovering the final 15 minutes. Remove from oven and let cool completely in the liquid. Chill, covered, several hours. Quarter the pears before serving.

Makes 16 pear quarters.

*Prosciutto and fruit—the
prosciutto ultra-thin and the
fruit ripe and cool—makes
a refreshingly simple appetizer.*

For Gingered Melons, luscious ripe fruit is poached in spiced wine and garnished with candied ginger. Whether you choose canteloupe or honeydew, give the melons an eye-catching shape with a stair-step "fan" cut (see opposite page).

GINGERED MELONS

Can you imagine a more refreshing appetizer? First simmered with ginger, then seasoned with pepper, these chilled melon fans make a particularly appealing partner to Asian-inspired hors d'oeuvres. Serve them in the height of summer with Teriyaki Chicken (see page 58), Peter Tamano's Twice-Fried Wings (see page 56), Pork Balls in Hoisin Sauce (see page 61), or Applewood-Smoked Beef (see page 55).

> 1 large or 2 small cantaloupe or honeydew melons, barely ripe
> 2 tablespoons minced crystallized ginger
> 2 tablespoons minced fresh ginger
> ½ cup rice wine
> Pinch sugar
> Pinch salt
> Half a cinnamon stick
> White pepper
> Lemon juice

1. Cut melons into fan shapes as shown on the opposite page.

2. In a small saucepan combine 1 tablespoon crystallized ginger, the fresh ginger, rice wine, sugar, salt, and cinnamon stick. Bring to a simmer. Add melon fans and simmer slowly for 1 to 2 minutes, depending on ripeness. (Less ripe melons will need to cook the longest.) Remove from heat and allow melons to cool in liquid.

3. Remove melons and strain liquid through a fine sieve. In a small saucepan over high heat, reduce liquid until syrupy. Pour over melons. To serve, season melons with a grinding of white pepper and a squeeze of lemon juice. Garnish with remaining crystallized ginger.

Makes 21 "fans."

GRILLED APPLES AND BRIE

Bread, cheese, and fruit—the foundation of many a picnic—make an appetizing trio when skewered and grilled. Although you *can* do the toasting under a broiler, a charcoal grill gives a far superior flavor.

   24 slices French baguette, each
       ¼ inch thick, lightly buttered
    4 ounces Brie, rind removed,
       cut into 16 slices
       approximately ⅛ inch thick
    1 large or 2 small firm apples,
       cored and sliced into 16 thin
       wedges
    2 tablespoons olive oil
    2 tablespoons butter, melted

1. Preheat broiler or grill. Thread a 6- to 8-inch skewer as follows: a piece of bread, cheese, apple, bread, cheese, apple, and bread. Press layers together firmly. Repeat with seven more skewers.

2. Combine olive oil and butter. Brush each skewer with oil-butter mixture, then broil or grill, turning frequently, until cheese begins to melt.

Makes 8 generous skewers.

Special Feature

TRICKS OF THE TRADE: MELON FANS

These fans are decoratively cut segments of melon. They may be incorporated into a fruit platter or salad; they make an attractive and refreshing accompaniment to barbecued or spicy food; or they can be a charming garnish. Or you can use the cutting technique to prepare fruit for recipes such as the Gingered Melons on the opposite page.

Cutting melon fans can be a bit tricky. You may find you need some practice to achieve satisfactory results. But once you get the hang of it, you'll enjoy the elegant effect they produce.

Start with a ripe melon. It can be any kind: cantaloupe, Crenshaw, honeydew, whatever is in season and looks luscious. Peel the melon, trying to produce a fairly smooth exterior. Cut it horizontally into 1-inch-thick rings; remove the seeds from the centers of the rings. Each ring will make 3 fans.

1. Cut melon ring into thirds.

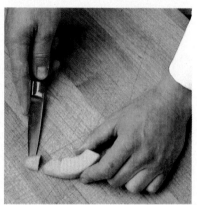

2. Holding the knife horizontally at a slight downward angle, cut into the end of one segment, beginning about a third of the way up, toward the other end. Angle the knife down and cut almost to the bottom of the melon slice. From the top, cut straight down to meet the first cut, being careful not to cut all the way through the slice. Remove the cut-out wedge.

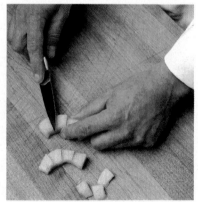

3. Continue to the end of the segment, making a stair-step series of cuts and removing the wedges.

CALIFORNIA HARVEST PLATTER

The juxtaposition of sweet and salty flavors makes for an appealing hors d'oeuvre, especially if the elements are California fruits and nuts. Wine-plumped prunes, salted almonds, and rosy ham complement one another and would be flattered by a sparkling wine or Riesling. The prunes marinate overnight; the almonds can be fried ahead, but they should be rewarmed in a hot oven just before serving.

- 12 California prunes, unpitted
- ½ cup California Cabernet Sauvignon
- 1 cinnamon stick
  Oil for deep-frying
- ½ pound raw unblanched almonds
  Kosher salt
- ½ pound best-quality ham, preferably pepper-cured or sugar-cured, thinly sliced

1. In a saucepan combine prunes, Cabernet Sauvignon, and cinnamon. Bring to a boil, then reduce heat and simmer 5 minutes. Remove from heat, cover, and let stand overnight. Discard cinnamon.

2. In a skillet or wok, heat 2 inches of vegetable oil to 375° F. Deep-fry almonds until lightly browned and fragrant; drain on paper towels and salt to taste.

3. At serving time, arrange prunes, warm nuts, and ham on a serving platter.

Serves 12.

Alternate Serving Suggestion

Use pitted prunes in place of unpitted prunes. Insert warm nuts in the cooled plumped prunes. Serve on a platter with sliced ham.

QUICK NO-COOK CHUTNEYS

There's more to "chutney" than Major Grey's. Indian chutneys are as diverse as the cooks who make them. They can be sweet, hot, mild, creamy, sour, thick, or thin; the common bond is that they're all used as a relish, a sort of counterpoint to the main event. The following "chutneys" are variations on the Indian theme, but with international applications.

Red Pepper and Cucumber Chutney

Here's a splendid relish for fish and shellfish—hot or cold, poached or fried. Try it with fried squid, cold prawns, steamed mussels, skewers of grilled salmon or Spice-Fried Halibut (see page 48).

- 2 pounds cucumbers, preferably English or Japanese variety
- 2 teaspoons kosher salt
- 1 large red bell pepper, halved, seeded, and minced
- 2 tablespoons minced shallot
- 1 tablespoon minced garlic
- ½ teaspoon dried hot red pepper flakes
- 2 tablespoons fresh lime juice
- ⅓ cup olive oil
- ½ tablespoon cider vinegar (optional)
  Sugar and salt to taste
- ¼ cup minced cilantro, dill, or mint (optional)

1. Peel cucumbers if they are not the thin-skinned English or Japanese varieties. Halve and seed them, then chop fine. Sprinkle with the kosher salt, then transfer to a colander and let drain 45 minutes.

2. Transfer cucumbers to a bowl. Add bell pepper, shallot, garlic, pepper flakes, lime juice, and olive oil. Stir to blend well. Taste; add vinegar if mixture needs more punch. Add sugar and salt to taste. Let rest in a cool place for 1 hour before serving. Just before serving, stir in minced cilantro (if used).

Makes 2½ cups.

Lime and Apple Chutney

Spoon it over skewered grilled chicken, shrimp, or pork, or present it as a dipping sauce.

- ½ cup fresh lime juice
- 2 tablespoons salt
- 1 onion, very finely minced
- 3 pounds Pippin or Granny Smith apples, peeled and chopped fine
- ½ teaspoon dried hot red pepper flakes
- 1 tablespoon honey
- ½ cup shredded unsweetened coconut

In a stainless steel, glass, or ceramic bowl, combine lime juice and salt and stir until salt is dissolved. Add onion, apples, hot pepper flakes, honey, and coconut. Stir to blend, then let rest at least 10 minutes before serving.

Makes about 4 cups.

Herb Chutney

This chutney makes a tasty basting sauce for skewers of grilled lamb, fish, or eggplant. Or stir some into yogurt to use as a dipping sauce for warm pita bread triangles or stuffed grape leaves.

- 1 cup minced fresh herbs (mint, parsley, dill, thyme, oregano)
  Half an onion, minced
- ¼ cup lemon juice
  Pinch each sugar and cayenne pepper
- 1¼ teaspoons salt
  Hot-pepper sauce to taste

Combine herbs, onion, lemon juice, sugar, cayenne, salt, and hot-pepper sauce in a bowl. Stir to blend, then let rest 1 hour at room temperature.

Makes 1 cup.

Tangy chutneys make tempting relishes for all kinds of food. From top, Herb, Red Pepper and Cucumber, and Lime and Apple.

PASTRY- AND BREAD-BASED HORS D'OEUVRES

Pastry- and bread-based hors d'oeuvres are an important category for cooks who entertain often, and it's not hard to see why. Most of the hors d'oeuvres that fall into this group are easy on guests. The bread or pastry makes a neat little package that can be eaten with ease. They are good choices for stand-up cocktail parties when you plan to pass all or most of the food.

What's more, these hors d'oeuvres are easy on the host, who can do much of the work in advance. Doughs and fillings can almost always be made ahead, then baked at the last minute. And many of the following selections can be fully baked ahead and successfully frozen.

To further please the host, pastry- and bread-based hors d'oeuvres are extraordinarily versatile. You can use the crust and change the filling or keep the filling but change the crust. Once you've mastered a basic tart dough, a brioche dough, or a blini batter, you can let your imagination and the market do the rest. For example, you probably won't want to make Polenta Tarts With Red-Pepper Filling (see page 76) in the depths of winter. The peppers would cost a fortune—if you could find them. Instead, why not substitute mushrooms or winter greens, which are then at their peak?

The best example of hors d'oeuvre versatility is certainly pizza. Although "making a pizza" is not synonymous with "cleaning out the fridge," it's true that many leftover bits and pieces can live again on a well-thought-out pie. As long as the flavors are complementary, the components fresh, and the cook judicious (more is

not better!), a good pizza is as near as the refrigerator shelf.

On the other hand, making pizza offers the chance to showcase the best in your market or garden. The first mushrooms, your homegrown tomatoes, your neighbor's zucchini— all can be strikingly mounted on pizza dough. Pizza and its cousin Focaccia (see page 87) may be new to the American cocktail table, but when cut in bite-sized squares or slender wedges, they make impressive party fare.

A PASTRY PRIMER

The aroma of bread or pastry baking is one of the most appetizing scents imaginable. To greet your guests with something fragrant and fresh from the oven is to ensure a good start to the evening. Here are the doughs with which you can build a repertoire of bread- and pastry-based hors d'oeuvres.

PÂTE À CHOUX
Cream puff paste

Choux paste is the foundation for two of the best known and most classic French pastries: éclairs and cream puffs. The fully baked puffs can also be filled with savory mixtures to make a variety of finger foods that are perfect for cocktails.

Despite appearances, this hollow puff is one of the easiest of all pastries to make. Because puffs are leavened by steam, it is important to keep the oven door closed during baking and to bake them until they are quite firm. Otherwise, they deflate during cooling as the steam pressure subsides.

Fully baked puffs can be frozen for several months. It is not a good idea to refrigerate unfilled puffs—either use them within a few hours or

freeze them. Nor should the dough be refrigerated; it must be used soon after mixing.

Puffs can be sliced in half and filled with sour cream and caviar, or they can be filled with a savory creamed mixture—like creamed crab or herbed cream cheese—using a pastry bag. When grated cheese is added to the pastry base, the result is *gougère*, one of the best of all possible companions for a glass of Beaujolais.

> 1 cup flour
> ⅛ teaspoon salt
> ½ cup milk
> ½ cup water
> ⅓ cup butter
> 4 or 5 eggs at room temperature

1. Preheat oven to 400° F. Sift together flour and salt. In a heavy saucepan combine milk, water, and butter and bring to a boil, adjusting heat so that butter is fully melted when mixture boils.

2. Add dry ingredients all at once, stirring constantly over low heat until smooth. The paste should leave the sides of the pan. Remove from heat and let cool 2 to 3 minutes.

3. Add 4 eggs, one at a time, beating well with a wooden spoon after each addition. Mixture should be firm and glossy. If it still looks dry, beat in the fifth egg.

4. Drop by heaping teaspoons onto a greased baking sheet, about 3 inches apart. Sprinkle dough lightly with a few drops of water. Bake 10 minutes, then reduce oven heat to 350° F and continue baking 25 minutes. Do not open oven door during first 15 minutes. Puffs should be brown and firm when done. Cool on a rack in a draft-free area.
Makes about 3 dozen 2-inch puffs.

Guests will love "gourmet" pizza—made, for example, with baby artichokes, fresh mushrooms, and mozzarella. Start with Pizza Dough (see page 72).

HOW TO MAKE PIZZA DOUGH

As specified in the recipe at right, pizza dough can be mixed by hand. However, to speed up the process, the initial mixing can also be done with a food processor, as shown in step 1.

1. *Process dough to lumpy state, not a smooth ball; do not overprocess. Finish mixing by hand.*

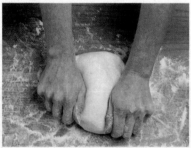

2. *Place dough on a lightly floured surface and knead until it is smooth and silky, adding more flour if necessary.*

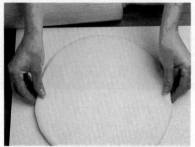

3. *On lightly floured surface, roll dough out to an even circle, ¼ inch thick, and place on tile.*

PIZZA DOUGH

A simple, straightforward dough enriched with oil, this one is ready to use in little more than an hour.

> *Half a package (1½ teaspoons) active dry yeast*
> ¾ *cup warm water (about 105° F)*
> 2 *tablespoons olive oil*
> 2½ *cups unbleached flour or bread flour*
> 1 *teaspoon salt*

1. In a small bowl dissolve yeast in the warm water and let proof 5 minutes. Stir in olive oil. In a large bowl combine flour and salt. Add yeast mixture and stir until dough just barely holds together.

2. Turn dough out on a lightly floured surface and knead until soft and silky, adding a little more flour if necessary. Put dough in an oiled bowl and turn to coat surface with oil. Cover bowl with plastic and let rise in a warm place until doubled, about 1 hour. Use dough in any of the pizza recipes (see pages 83-86).

Makes enough dough for 12 to 15 cocktail wedges or 20 to 24 small squares.

PÂTE BRISÉE

Pâte brisée is the basic French tart dough. It is buttery, nonsweet, and, when properly mixed, tender and flaky. The key to a tender pie crust is to work the dough lightly. Using chilled butter and ice-cold water also helps. To avoid "shrinking" during baking, chill the dough before rolling it out and again in the tart tins before baking.

Tart rings and tins are sold in a wide range of sizes, all of which can be used for hors d'oeuvres. The tiny 2-inch "tartlet" tins, which are ideal for making finger foods, are recommended for the recipes in this chapter. If you choose a custard- or quiche-type filling that will slice well when baked, you can use larger tart tins (4-inch, 8-inch, and 9-inch are common sizes) and cut the finished tart into appetizer-sized wedges; however, none of the recipes in this chapter is suitable for large tins.

Pâte brisée tarts can be the basis for a thousand different hors d'oeuvres. The dough is so useful, in fact, that it makes sense to have some always on hand. You can freeze it, then thaw it overnight in the refrigerator. You can also freeze unbaked tart shells in their tins, well covered with foil. Or you can freeze partially baked shells in plastic bags. Bake them "blind" in a preheated 400° F oven directly from the freezer, or fill the shells directly from the freezer and let them finish baking along with the filling.

The recipe below can be doubled. However, if you are using a food processor, do not make a double batch unless you have a large work bowl. A double batch is easily overworked in a small processor, resulting in tough pastry.

> 2 *cups unbleached flour*
> 1 *teaspoon salt*
> ½ *cup plus 2 tablespoons unsalted butter, cut into small pieces and frozen for 30 minutes*
> 1 *egg mixed with 1 tablespoon cold water*

1. Combine flour and salt in a bowl. Cut in butter until mixture resembles coarse crumbs. Add egg-water mixture and mix only until dough just holds together.

2. Pat dough out on a lightly floured surface into a rectangle approximately 6 inches by 8 inches, wrap in plastic, and chill at least an hour.

3. Preheat oven to 375° F. On a lightly floured surface, roll dough out ¹⁄₁₆ inch thick. With a floured 3-inch cutter, cut out rounds. Press into tartlet tins with fingertips and prick with a fork. For a partially baked shell, bake about 10 minutes; for fully baked, bake 5 to 8 minutes more.

Makes about 2 dozen 2-inch shells.

QUICK AND EASY PUFF PASTRY

Making classic French puff pastry is *never* a "quick and easy" job. Achieving its thousand flaky layers is a fairly tedious process. There's no denying its miraculous lightness, but using the quick method outlined below, you can get very similar results with half the effort. The finished product is exceptionally light and flaky, suitable for tarts, twists, and turnovers. The dough may be frozen, well wrapped, for several months, or refrigerated for up to three days. If it is frozen, thaw in refrigerator overnight before using.

1⅓   cups all-purpose flour
⅔   cup cake or pastry flour
1   teaspoon salt
14   tablespoons unsalted
      butter, cut in pieces and
      frozen for 30 minutes
½ to ¾ cup very cold
      whipping cream

1. Combine flours and salt in a bowl or on a marble work surface. Cut in butter coarsely until it is reduced to ¼-inch bits. Add ½ cup cream and mix gently, adding additional cream if necessary, until mixture just forms a ball. Amount of cream will vary depending on humidity and type of flour.

2. Roll dough out on a lightly floured surface into a rectangle measuring approximately 8 by 20 inches. Fold the two 8-inch ends toward the center until they meet in the middle. Then fold one half over the other (see photographs on opposite page). Wrap in plastic and refrigerate dough 1 hour. Repeat the rolling and folding process twice, refrigerating the dough 1 hour after each time. Repeat rolling and folding one more time. Puff pastry is now ready to use.

Makes about 1 pound puff pastry, enough for 15 bouchées (see page 82) or 4 dozen palmiers (see page 80).

Basics

HOW TO MAKE PUFF PASTRY

Making puff pastry doesn't have to be a tedious and intimidating process. Follow the recipe at left and you can easily make delicious pastry with only a modest investment of time. This quick method is like the classical one in that it calls for repeated rolling, folding, and turning; the difference is in how the butter is incorporated into the dough.

Puff Pastry has many uses. Try it in Poppy Seed Spirals (see page 79) or Palmiers (see page 80). It is also used to make the flaky morsels called Bouchées. A recipe for Creamy Mushroom and Liver Bouchées is on page 82, and one for Bouchées Dijonnaises appears on page 92, as part of the New Year's Eve menu.

For this recipe, as with other pastry doughs, a marble work surface is best.

1. *On work surface, using hands, combine flours and salt; cut in butter and add cream. Dough does not have to be perfectly smooth; a few particles of butter may still remain.*

2. *With one 8-inch end of rolled-out dough near you, fold the two 8-inch ends of the dough to the center.*

3. *Fold one side over the other, trying to make a square, even packet with ends meeting.*

73

HOW TO MAKE BRIOCHES

The traditional brioche is a rich breakfast bread. It is made of two pieces of dough, a base and a smaller "top-knot," that readily separate after it has been baked to produce a little nest just right for a spoonful of jam. It is baked in a medium-sized fluted tin as shown here.

However, the versatile brioche dough may also be baked in a single large fluted tin or in a large buttered loaf pan, to be sliced and, perhaps, toasted. In addition, there are tiny brioche tins, for bite-sized versions.

For entertaining, brioches—no matter what their size or shape—can be served as tasty nibbles on their own, or they can be filled with something savory (see suggestions in the introduction to the recipe at right).

1. *Dough rises in a buttered bowl until doubled, about 1½ hours.*

2. *After dividing dough into 24 large balls and 24 small balls, place large balls in buttered brioche tins. With floured thumb, make an indentation in top of each and place a small ball in each indentation.*

3. *Brush egg-cream glaze over dough, being careful not to get any glaze on tins.*

QUICK AND EASY BRIOCHE DOUGH

Buttery brioches—the little golden buns crowned with topknots—are one of the glories of French breakfast tables, to be eaten on special mornings—with plenty of jam.

But a brioche also makes an elegant package for savory fillings. For hors d'oeuvres, make the brioches small (about 24 from the following recipe). After baking, remove the top-knot, pull out some of the crumb, and fill the space with a nugget of warm chicken or duck liver; a spoonful of creamed chicken, lobster, or mushrooms; or creamy scrambled eggs with chives. The dough can also be baked in a large loaf pan, then cooled, sliced, and toasted. Warm toasted brioche is a splendid accompaniment to almost any pâté. Real French brioches are baked in small, fluted tins, available in most kitchenware shops.

The following recipe is designed for use with a food processor. Brioche dough can be made by hand, but it must be kneaded very thoroughly and is then no longer "quick and easy."

> ¼ cup warm whipping cream (about 105° F)
> ½ teaspoon sugar
> 1 package active dry yeast
> 2 cups flour
> 1 teaspoon salt
> 3 eggs at room temperature
> ½ cup butter, melted and cooled
> 1 or 2 egg yolks (see steps 4 and 5)
> 1 or 2 tablespoons whipping cream (see steps 4 and 5)

1. Combine cream and sugar, then add yeast and stir briskly to dissolve. Let proof 5 minutes.

2. Put yeast mixture and remaining ingredients in food processor fitted with the steel blade. Process 10 seconds. Turn dough out on a lightly floured surface and knead by hand, adding more flour as necessary to make a supple, soft, but manageable dough. It should adhere only slightly to your hand.

3. Transfer dough to a buttered bowl and turn to coat all sides with butter. Cover with plastic and set aside to rise 1½ hours or until doubled. Punch dough down with a lightly floured fist.

4. *To bake in 2-inch brioche tins:* Preheat oven to 400° F. Divide dough into two unequal portions—one third and two thirds. Then divide each portion into 24 balls. Place larger balls in 24 buttered brioche tins. With a floured thumb make an indentation in each larger ball. Nestle a small ball in each indentation. Let rise until doubled. Whisk together 2 egg yolks and 2 tablespoons cream. Brush brioches with half of the egg glaze, being careful not to let glaze touch sides of tins. Repeat 5 minutes later with remaining glaze. Bake 10 minutes, then reduce oven heat to 350° F and bake until golden brown (about 5 to 10 minutes more).

5. *To bake in loaf shape:* Preheat oven to 400° F. Form dough into a loaf shape. Place in a buttered 9-inch loaf pan. Let rise until doubled. Whisk together 1 egg yolk and 1 tablespoon cream. Brush dough with half of the egg glaze, being careful not to let glaze touch sides of pan. Repeat 5 minutes later with remaining glaze. Bake 10 minutes, then reduce oven to 350° F and continue baking 30 minutes longer or until loaf sounds hollow when tapped on the bottom. Remove from pan and cool completely on a rack before slicing. Brioche dough can also be baked in a buttered 1-pound coffee can if round slices are preferred.

Makes about 2 dozen tiny brioches or one 9-inch loaf.

Make-Ahead Tip Dough can be made a day ahead. After rising, punch down, cover, and refrigerate overnight. Shape dough while still cold. Because dough is cold, second rising will take longer.

COCKTAIL BLINI

Yeast-risen buckwheat pancakes were a fixture on the tables of imperial Russia, served dripping with butter and caviar, or with sour cream and smoked fish. Made in a smaller cocktail size, they are novel and fun and can be topped in many different ways: with sour cream and chutney; with sour cream herring; with crème fraîche and smoked trout; with a slice of grilled sausage; with melted herb butter and tiny shrimp; with melted butter and smoked oysters. Serve piping hot, with chilled vodka, Champagne, or cocktails.

> 1 *package active dry yeast*
> 2 *cups scalded milk, cooled to 105° F*
> 2 *tablespoon sugar*
> 1½ *cups buckwheat flour*
> 3 *eggs, separated*
> 6 *tablespoons butter, softened*
> 1½ *cups all-purpose flour*
> ¾ *teaspoon salt*

1. Dissolve yeast in milk and let proof 5 minutes. Add sugar and buckwheat flour. Beat well. Place in a well-oiled bowl, cover with a warm damp towel, and let rise 2 hours.

2. Add egg yolks, butter, all-purpose flour, and salt. Beat well, then cover and let rise another 2 hours.

3. Whip egg whites until stiff but not dry; gently fold into batter.

4. Heat a nonstick griddle or skillet until it almost smokes. Drop batter onto skillet by large tablespoons. Batter will puff up slightly. When blini are browned on one side, turn and cook an additional 30 to 45 seconds until browned on second side. Serve hot!

Makes about 2 dozen blini.

BRIOCHE GALETTES WITH ARTICHOKES, HAM, AND OLIVES

A variation on the pizza theme, these *galettes* (flat cakes) are made with rounds of brioche dough. Garnish them however you like, but avoid creamy or runny mixtures, for the rounds are small and rimless.
In this colorful version, pale green hearts of artichoke contrast with smoky pink ham. Use the small egg-sized artichokes, which have the most tender hearts.

> *Quick and Easy Brioche Dough (see opposite page)*
> 3 *small artichokes*
> *Half a lemon*
> ¼ *cup olive oil*
> 1 *cup julienned smoked ham*
> 1 *cup mixed green and black olives, pitted*
> ½ *cup freshly grated Parmesan cheese*
> ¼ *cup minced parsley*

1. Divide brioche dough into 12 equal balls. Roll each ball into a round, about 2½ inches in diameter. Transfer to lightly greased baking sheets and let rise until doubled.

2. Trim stem ends of artichokes and peel off outer leaves until only the pale green "heart" remains. Rub all over with lemon. Cook hearts in boiling salted water until tender when pierced with the tip of a small, sharp knife. Cool slightly, then quarter. Remove any fuzzy "choke" in the center.

3. Preheat oven to 375° F. Brush brioche rounds lightly with 2 tablespoons of the olive oil. Make a slight depression in the center of each round and place a quarter-heart in each depression. Arrange ham and olives around the artichokes. Drizzle with remaining oil and dust with Parmesan. Bake until well browned. Cool slightly. Serve garnished with minced parsley.

Makes 1 dozen galettes.

PUMPKIN SATCHELS

A savory cream cheese pastry surrounds a harvest-time filling of eggplant, Brazil nuts, and pumpkin. Pile the golden "satchels" in a handsome fall basket or mound them on a delicate doily-lined platter. A glass of sherry would complement their nutty goodness.

Pastry

- ½ cup butter, at room temperature
- 9 ounces cream cheese, at room temperature
- 1½ cups flour

Filling

- 3 tablespoons butter
- 1 large onion, finely chopped
- ½ cup mashed cooked eggplant
- ½ cup chopped Brazil nuts
- 1 cup diced (about ¼-inch dice) cooked pumpkin
- ¼ teaspoon dried thyme
- ½ teaspoon salt
  Freshly ground black pepper to taste
- 2 tablespoons flour
- ¼ cup sour cream

1. *To prepare pastry:* In an electric mixer or by hand, cream butter and cream cheese. Add flour and beat until smooth. Chill dough at least 30 minutes.

2. *To prepare filling:* In a heavy skillet over medium heat, melt butter. Add onion and sauté until lightly browned. Add eggplant, nuts, and pumpkin and sauté 3 minutes, stirring often. Add thyme, salt, and pepper. Sprinkle flour over surface of filling. Stir in sour cream and cook gently until thickened.

3. *To assemble satchels:* Preheat oven to 450° F. Roll dough out to ⅛-inch thickness on a lightly floured surface. Use a 3-inch biscuit cutter to cut as many rounds as possible. Re-roll scraps and cut additional rounds.

Place a teaspoon of filling on each round and fold dough over the filling. Press edges together with a fork. Prick tops to allow steam to escape. Bake satchels on ungreased baking sheets for about 15 minutes or until lightly browned.

Makes about 2 dozen satchels.

CORN CLOUDS WITH SPICY SALSA

Fluffy cornmeal batter turns into buttery corn "clouds" to be topped with sour cream and salsa. Or put a platter of these dollar-sized "clouds" beside a selection of garnishes—cubed avocados, chopped tomatoes, marinated red onion slices, chopped red pepper, chopped green onion—and let guests help themselves. Serve when fresh corn is at its peak, as a partner to cocktails or cold Mexican beer.

- 1½ cups flour
- ½ cup cornmeal
- 1 teaspoon baking powder
- 6 eggs, separated
- 6 ounces cream cheese
- 1½ cups milk
- ½ cup unsalted butter, melted
- ¼ cup minced green onion
- 1 cup corn kernels cut fresh from cob
- 1 teaspoon salt
  Hot-pepper sauce to taste
  Butter and corn oil for frying
  Salsa Verde (see page 51)
  Sour cream

1. Sift together flour, cornmeal, and baking powder. In large bowl of electric mixer, cream egg yolks and cream cheese. Add cornmeal mixture, then slowly add milk. Stir in melted butter, green onions, corn kernels, salt, and hot-pepper sauce to taste.

2. In a separate bowl beat egg whites with a pinch of salt until they are stiff but not dry. Fold one third of whites into batter. Then gently fold batter into remaining whites.

3. Grease a nonstick frying pan with 1 teaspoon each butter and corn oil. Heat pan until butter foams. Drop batter into hot fat by rounded tablespoons and cook until bubbles form and burst on top. Turn cakes over and cook an additional 30 seconds. Transfer cakes to a warm platter and dot with salsa, sour cream, or both.

Makes about 5 dozen dollar-sized cakes.

POLENTA TARTS WITH RED-PEPPER FILLING

A polenta shell filled with a sweet red-pepper purée and topped with two Italian cheeses makes a perfect companion to a bottle of Soave, or an excellent preface to an Italian meal. Shells and filling can be made several hours ahead, then combined and baked just before guests arrive.

Tart Shells

- 4 cups water
- 1 teaspoon salt
- 1 cup polenta (coarse-grained cornmeal)
- 8 tablespoons butter

Filling

- 1 cup olive oil
- 5 to 6 large red bell peppers, halved, seeded, and deribbed, then cut into long thin strips
- 3 cloves garlic, minced
- 2 tablespoons chopped fresh oregano, or 1 tablespoon dried
  Salt and black pepper
  Hot-pepper sauce (optional)
- 3 egg yolks
- 4 ounces whole-milk ricotta cheese
- ⅛ cup grated fontina or mozzarella cheese
- ⅛ cup freshly grated Parmesan cheese

1. *To prepare tart shells:* Bring water and salt to a boil in a heavy-bottomed saucepan. Gradually add polenta and cook for 20 minutes over moderate heat, stirring frequently to prevent mixture from lumping or sticking to the bottom of the pan. Mixture will thicken considerably. Remove from heat. Stir in butter, a tablespoon at a time. Let sit until cool enough to handle. Put about 2 tablespoons of the mixture into each 2-inch muffin or tartlet tin. Press mixture evenly up the sides, then allow to cool until quite firm. If you make the shells a few hours ahead, do not refrigerate, but keep in a cool place.

2. *To prepare filling:* Preheat oven to 400° F. Heat ½ cup of the olive oil in a large skillet. Add peppers, garlic, and oregano. Cook over medium heat, covered, for 15 minutes. Remove from heat. Season to taste with salt, pepper, and hot-pepper sauce (if used). Purée peppers in a food processor or food mill. If you use a processor, sieve the mixture after puréeing. Whisk in the remaining oil, then add egg yolks and ricotta. Divide this mixture among the cornmeal shells. Dust tops with the two cheeses and bake 20 minutes. Let tarts rest 5 minutes before serving. To remove tarts from muffin tins, run a sharp knife around the edge and lift out.

Makes 2 dozen 2-inch tarts.

Airy Corn Clouds are light enough to float, worth making only with fresh, sweet summer corn. Pan-fried in butter, they're topped with sour cream—a novel offering that's pretty close to irresistible.

Serve yeast-raised Cocktail Crumpets hot, with smoked meats, a wedge of Cheddar, mustard, and chutney.

CABBAGE TOURTE

If you are fond of braised cabbage with apples and caraway, you'll like it even better layered with flaky strudel leaves. Serve warm squares of this German specialty with a glass of Riesling, or serve at room temperature with a dollop of sour cream.

1½ cups unsalted butter
1 large onion, minced, or ⅓ cup minced shallots
1 pound shredded green cabbage, or mixed red and green cabbage
¼ cup red wine vinegar
1 tart green apple, peeled, cored, and coarsely grated
Salt and black pepper to taste
½ cup fresh bread crumbs
2 teaspoons caraway seed
4 eggs, lightly beaten
4 ounces grated Muenster or Monterey jack cheese
16 sheets filo dough

1. In a large skillet over medium heat, melt ½ cup of the butter. Add onion and cook over moderate heat 3 to 5 minutes, stirring. Add cabbage and cook 5 minutes, uncovered. Add vinegar, apple, salt, and pepper. Cover and continue cooking 20 to 25 minutes or until cabbage is wilted and soft. Cool completely. Taste and adjust seasoning.

2. Combine cabbage with ¼ cup of the crumbs, caraway seed, eggs, and cheese. Mix well and set aside.

3. Preheat oven to 375° F. Generously butter an 11- by 13- by 2-inch baking pan. Melt the remaining 1 cup butter. Set out filo sheets, covered with clean, well-wrung-out cloth to keep them from drying out. Lay one sheet of filo on the baking sheet. Brush lightly with melted butter. Repeat with 4 more leaves of filo dough, brushing each sheet with melted butter. Spread cabbage mixture over last layer. Layer the remaining filo leaves on top of the cabbage, brushing each layer with butter and sprinkling a bit of the remaining bread crumbs between layers.

4. Cut strudel into 40 squares or into diamonds. Bake 30 minutes or until top is golden. Cool slightly before serving.

Makes about 40 squares.

Make-Ahead Tip Step 1 can be completed a day ahead.

COCKTAIL CRUMPETS

What would an English tea table be without crumpets and jam? Toasted crumpets are a fixture there, but they also fit right in with American cocktails. Make them smaller and serve them toasted and buttered, along with smoked meats or sliced Cheddar and an assortment of chutneys. They can be made early in the day, then grilled, toasted, or reheated in a 350° F oven just before serving.

1 package active dry yeast
1 teaspoon sugar
¾ cup warm water (about 105° F)
¾ teaspoon salt
2 tablespoons unsalted butter, melted
½ cup milk, scalded and cooled to room temperature
1¼ cups unbleached flour
½ teaspoon baking soda
1 tablespoon boiling water

1. Dissolve yeast and sugar in the warm water. Let proof 10 minutes. Then add salt, butter, and milk and mix well. Add flour all at once and beat steadily for at least 4 minutes. Cover with a warm damp towel and let rise in a warm place until doubled.

2. Combine baking soda with the boiling water. Add to batter and stir until completely blended. Cover and let rise again until doubled.

3. Lightly butter crumpet rings (you can also use clean, empty tin cans, 6½- to 7-ounce size, with both ends removed). Heat a nonstick griddle or skillet. Place rings or cans on skillet. Put a rounded tablespoon of batter in each. (Alternatively, you can make them without rings in a rustic, free-form style. Then, if you like, trim the cooked crumpets with a biscuit cutter to make them uniform.)

4. Cover skillet and cook until a light crust forms on top, about 5 minutes. Remove cover and turn crumpets. Cook a few minutes more, uncovered, to brown second side.

Makes about 2 dozen crumpets.

POPPY SEED SPIRALS

These flaky little twists can be made in a flash if you keep Quick and Easy Puff Pastry on hand in the freezer. However, as specified in step 1, they should rest at least an hour between rolling and baking. Don't hesitate to try variations: Replace the poppy seed with toasted sesame seed or with a little coarse salt and cayenne pepper. Mound the spirals in a basket or on a doily-lined tray and serve warm with cocktails. They also make a lovely partner to first-course soups.

Quick and Easy Puff Pastry (see page 73)
1 cup poppy seed

1. On a surface covered with the poppy seed, roll dough into a rectangle about 4 inches wide, 16 inches long, and ⅛ inch thick. Cut rectangle into strips ⅓ inch wide. Twist strips into spirals. Place spirals on ungreased cookie sheets and freeze 1 hour or refrigerate 3 to 4 hours.

2. Preheat oven to 375° F. Bake spirals 25 to 30 minutes or until golden. Serve warm, or cool completely and store in an airtight tin for up to 1 month.

Makes about 50 spirals.

HOW TO MAKE PALMIERS

Palmiers can be made with Parmesan, as shown here, or with sugar for a sweet pastry.

1. *With long edge of rolled-out dough facing you, fold 8-inch sides into center, then fold one end over the other, making edges meet.*

2. *With last fold facing you, slice chilled dough in ¼-inch widths.*

3. *Place slices on ungreased baking sheets, widely spaced.*

CHEESE PALMIERS

Dainty *palmiers* ("palm leaves"), made with puff pastry, are sold in almost every French pastry shop. Rolled in sugar, they are eaten with dessert; when rolled in salt or grated cheese, they become a savory, to enjoy with cocktails or wine.

> *Quick and Easy Puff Pastry (see page 73)*
> 1½ cups freshly grated Parmesan cheese

1. On a surface covered with the grated Parmesan, roll out puff pastry dough into a rectangle 8 inches wide, 12 inches long, and ⅛ inch thick.

2. Fold the two 8-inch sides toward the center, meeting in the middle (see photo at left). Dust surface lightly with cheese. Then fold top half of dough down over bottom half. Dust dough with any remaining Parmesan. Chill dough, wrapped in plastic, for 1 hour.

3. Preheat oven to 350° F. Cut roll into ¼-inch widths. Place on ungreased baking sheets, widely separated. Bake 20 to 25 minutes or until golden brown. Serve warm, or cool on a rack and store in an airtight container for up to 2 weeks.

Makes about 50 palmiers.

SEVEN-ONION CREAM TARTS

There are seven—count them, seven—members of the onion family in these tarts, but slow cooking and a finishing of cream and cheese render them sweet and mild. These are delicate tartlets, picture pretty, to present on a silver tray.

> ½ cup unsalted butter
> ½ cup minced red onion
> ½ cup minced white onion
> ⅓ pound pearl onions, peeled
> 1 shallot, minced
> 2 green onions, minced
> 3 cloves garlic, minced
> ½ cup dry white wine
> ½ cup whipping cream
> ¼ cup freshly grated Parmesan cheese
> 2 tablespoons minced chives
> Salt and black pepper
> 24 partially baked 2-inch tartlet shells (see Pâte Brisée, page 72)

1. Preheat oven to 375° F. In a large, heavy skillet over medium heat, melt butter. Add red onion, white onion, pearl onions, shallot, green onion, and garlic. Cook over medium heat until onions are softened, about 15 minutes.

2. Add wine, increase heat, and cook until only 2 tablespoons of liquid remain. Add cream and reduce over moderately high heat until mixture is thick. Remove from heat; stir in Parmesan and chives. Add salt and black pepper to taste.

3. Divide mixture among tartlet shells. Bake 10 to 12 minutes, then glaze briefly under a preheated broiler, watching constantly. Cool slightly before serving.

Makes 2 dozen tartlets.

GARLIC AND LEEK TARTLETS

Creamy braised leeks laced with garlic purée make a filling that's not for the faint-hearted. "Garlic heads" will adore these dainty tartlets; others can double the leeks and omit the *Allium sativum.* Fully baked tartlets freeze well for up to three months; reheat directly from the freezer. You can also freeze them unbaked in the tart tins. Extra filling freezes well for up to two months.

> 2 heads garlic, broken up into cloves and peeled
> 1 cup water
> 1⅓ cups whipping cream
> ½ cup butter, softened
> 3 to 4 medium leeks
> Salt and pepper to taste
> 4 egg yolks
> 24 partially baked 2-inch tartlet shells (see Pâte Brisée, page 72)
> ⅓ cup freshly grated Parmesan cheese

1. In a heavy saucepan combine garlic cloves, water, and 1 cup of the cream. Bring to a boil, then reduce heat and simmer very slowly for 1 hour, or until garlic is very tender. You may need to add more water if mixture cooks dry before cloves are soft enough.

2. Purée softened garlic in a food processor or blender. Transfer to a bowl and stir in 2 tablespoons softened butter.

3. Preheat oven to 375° F. Clean the leeks thoroughly; trim root end and remove all but 1 inch of green ends. Slice leeks into thin rounds. In a large skillet, melt remaining 6 tablespoons butter. Add leeks, salt, and pepper, and cook over moderate heat for about 20 minutes, stirring occasionally, or until leeks are quite tender. Add remaining ⅓ cup cream and continue cooking until mixture reduces to a thick and creamy mass. Remove from heat.

4. Combine leeks and puréed garlic. Add egg yolks and mix well.

5. Spoon a little filling into each tartlet shell. Dust each tart lightly with Parmesan, then place on a heavy baking sheet and bake until browned and slightly puffed, 10 to 12 minutes. Cool briefly before serving.

Makes about 2 dozen tartlets.

TARTITAS AZTECAS

Authentic? Maybe not, but they *are* delectable: flour tortillas stacked with chiles and cheese, then bound with a creamy custard. Bake these spicy mouthfuls in muffin tins and serve hot with ice-cold beer or margaritas.

> 18 small (6- to 8-inch) flour tortillas
> 12 ounces cream cheese
> ¾ teaspoon cayenne pepper, or to taste
> 8 ounces chopped mild green chiles, canned and drained, or fresh, roasted and peeled
> 3 eggs

> 1 teaspoon salt
> 1½ cups whipping cream
> 1 cup grated Monterey jack cheese
> Salsa Verde (see page 51)

1. Preheat oven to 375° F. Using a 2-inch biscuit cutter, cut 36 rounds out of tortillas. Place 12 rounds in well-oiled muffin tins.

2. Combine cream cheese and cayenne. Put about a tablespoon on each tortilla round and top with a little of the chopped chile. Cover each with another tortilla round.

3. Blend eggs, salt, and cream. Spoon 2 tablespoons into each muffin tin. Cover with remaining tortilla rounds. Sprinkle each with grated cheese.

4. Bake tartitas 20 to 25 minutes or until well browned. Cool slightly and serve with Salsa Verde.

Makes 1 dozen tartitas.

Quick puff pastry dusted with Parmesan can be turned into buttery Cheese Palmiers, to serve warm or cool with cocktails or red wine. Provide plates or large napkins; the palmiers are deliciously flaky!

An oven-baked egg nestled in butter-rich brioche makes a perfect first course for an elegant dinner. Don't hesitate to gild the lily with a dot of caviar and a glass of chilled Champagne.

BRIOCHE WITH BAKED EGGS

Why didn't *we* think of this? Inspired by cookbook author Paula Wolfert, buttery brioche and eggs are combined here in a delightfully surprising fashion. The golden brioches are hollowed out, an egg is slipped into the resultant "nest," and the whole is baked until the egg just sets. Nap the egg with saffron cream or spoon on a dot of caviar and you have an elegant first course, best eaten with a knife and fork. For finger food, halve the size of the brioches, bake them in 2-inch fluted tins, scoop them out, and bake a quail egg inside.

> *Quick and Easy Brioche Dough (see page 74)*
> 2 *egg yolks*
> 1 *tablespoon whipping cream*
> 12 *eggs*
> 6 *tablespoons butter*
> *Salt and black pepper*
> *Saffron Hollandaise (see page 51) or caviar (optional)*

1. Shape brioche dough into 24 balls, 12 large and 12 small, following the directions on page 74, and place in buttered 3-inch brioche tins. Let rise until dough fills molds and is springy to the touch.

2. Preheat oven to 450° F. Combine egg yolks and cream. Lightly brush tops and sides of dough with egg glaze. Bake 5 minutes, then lower heat to 350° F and continue baking until done, about 10 minutes. Remove from tins and cool on a rack.

3. When brioches are cool, scoop out the insides, leaving a sturdy wall (reserve crumbs for another use—stuffings, meat loaves, or casserole toppings; or you can eat them fresh and hot with butter and jam).

4. Lightly butter insides of brioche shells, then drop an egg into each hollow. Dot each egg with a teaspoon of butter; salt and pepper to taste. Bake until eggs are just set, 10 to 15 minutes. Serve hot, topped with Saffron Hollandaise or caviar, if desired.

Makes 1 dozen brioches.

CREAMY MUSHROOM AND LIVER BOUCHÉES

Bouchée is the French word for "little mouthful," which is just what these are: little mouthfuls of flaky pastry with fillings. Bouchées are a useful part of the hors d'oeuvre repertoire, for they can be garnished with just about anything—in this case, a Madeira-scented mushroom-and-liver filling; other possibilities might be creamed chicken or sweetbreads, curried crab or shrimp, sautéed mushrooms, or creamed asparagus. This particular filling can be made a day ahead and refrigerated, or made several weeks ahead and frozen. Thaw and reheat before filling bouchées. The pastry can be baked several hours before filling.

*Quick and Easy Puff Pastry
(see page 73)*

14 tablespoons butter
2 shallots, minced
1 pound mushrooms, cleaned
and minced
½ pound chicken livers, trimmed
of all fat and coarsely
chopped
3 tablespoons Madeira
1 tablespoon whipping cream
Salt and black pepper
¼ cup minced parsley

1. Preheat oven to 475° F. Roll puff pastry dough ¼ inch thick on a lightly floured surface. Cut out rounds with a 2-inch biscuit cutter. Use a small sharp knife or a 1-inch biscuit cutter to mark small *"lids"* on half of the 2-inch rounds. Brush the unmarked 2-inch rounds lightly with cold water. Position the marked rounds directly on top. Transfer to baking sheets and bake 5 minutes, then reduce heat to 400° F and bake an additional 5 to 8 minutes or until done. Cool bouchées on a rack. When cool, remove the lids and scoop out the soft centers.

2. Melt ½ cup (8 tablespoons) of the butter in a large skillet over moderate heat. Add shallots and cook 3 minutes, or until shallots begin to soften. Add mushrooms and cook 20 minutes, or until mushroom liquid has almost completely evaporated. Set aside.

3. In a separate skillet melt the remaining 6 tablespoons butter. Add the livers and cook just until they lose their raw, pink look. Add Madeira and cook 30 seconds. Add cream and remove from heat.

4. Combine mushrooms and livers. Season to taste with salt and pepper. Stir in half the parsley. Divide mixture among the bouchées. Reheat in a 400° F oven 5 to 7 minutes. Serve warm, garnished with remaining parsley.

Makes about 15 bouchées.

PIZZA

Pizza before dinner? Absolutely! Many dishes that would make a full dinner if served in large portions—like pizza—make tempting hors d'oeuvres when served in small cocktail "bites." If you keep the topping light and fragrant and avoid the temptation to make an inch-thick layer of toppings, your pizza can be as appetite-arousing as any canapé.

Making pizza at home is no more difficult than baking bread. All you need is a hot oven and, for best results, a baking stone. You can buy a 12-inch-square terra-cotta tile at just about any tile supply store. Set it on your oven's lower rack and preheat it at least 30 minutes in a 450° F oven. Shape and garnish your pizza on a well-floured inverted baking sheet, then slide it onto the preheated stone. Because the tile holds heat so well, the pizza dough browns beautifully and turns deliciously crisp and crusty.

The following recipes demonstrate the notion that the best hors d'oeuvre pizzas are simple ones. Because they are simple, however, they require the best ingredients:

☐ Use a good virgin or extra-virgin olive oil.

☐ Buy blocks of imported Parmesan cheese and grate just before using.

☐ Use fresh mozzarella if available; otherwise use a premium brand of packaged mozzarella, not presliced.

☐ Use fresh herbs when possible.

☐ Use *only* fresh garlic, chopped shortly before using. Garlic salt and garlic powder are not acceptable substitutes.

PIZZA ALL' AGLIO, OLIO, ED OREFANO
Pizza with garlic, oil, and oregano

By American standards, this would hardly classify as pizza. Where are the tomatoes and cheese? The Sicilians know you don't need tomatoes to make a pizza, especially when the new spring garlic crop is in.

Because this pizza is so simple, it requires the best ingredients. Use only young, nonsprouting spring garlic, virgin olive oil, and fresh oregano (in Sicily, it's called *orefano*). You can dress up this pizza with chopped clams, shrimp, or roasted red peppers, if you wish.

*Pizza Dough (see
page 72)*
6 cloves young garlic, minced
very fine
Olive oil
½ cup dry white wine
2 tablespoons chopped fresh
oregano
*Salt and black pepper
Freshly grated Parmesan
cheese (optional)*

1. Preheat baking stone at least 30 minutes in a 450° F oven (or in a 475° F oven for a crisper crust). Roll pizza dough into a square or round and place on a well-floured inverted baking sheet.

2. In a small saucepan over low heat, cook garlic, ¼ cup of the olive oil, and wine until garlic is very soft, about 45 minutes. You will be left with a rough paste. Spread the paste on the pizza dough. Drizzle with more olive oil and sprinkle with oregano. Season with salt and pepper.

3. Slide pizza onto heated baking stone; bake until well browned and puffy, about 20 minutes. Dust with Parmesan (if used), cut into squares or wedges, and serve hot.

Makes 12 to 15 cocktail wedges or 20 to 24 small squares.

ARTICHOKE AND MUSHROOM PIZZA

This recipe calls for "baby" artichokes, which are about the size of a small egg and have a very tender heart. If you can't get these tiny artichokes fresh, buy frozen hearts, but do not parboil them. Thaw them and marinate a few hours in a mixture of olive oil, lemon juice, and chopped fresh herbs. Then quarter and use as directed.

> Pizza Dough (see page 72)
> 6 "baby" artichokes
> Half a lemon
> 1 bay leaf
> 6 peppercorns
> ½ cup white wine
> ½ pound mushrooms, thinly sliced
> ¾ cup freshly grated Parmesan cheese
> ⅓ cup grated whole-milk mozzarella cheese
> ½ cup finely minced green onion
> Freshly ground black pepper
> Olive oil

1. Preheat baking stone at least 30 minutes in a 450° F oven (or in a 475° F oven for a crisper crust). Roll pizza dough into a square or round and place on a well-floured inverted baking sheet.

2. Trim stem ends of artichokes and peel off outer leaves until only the pale green "heart" remains. Rub all over with lemon, then put lemon, bay leaf, peppercorns, and wine in a pot with plenty of water. Bring to a boil, add artichoke hearts, and parboil 5 to 6 minutes or until almost tender. Drain; quarter the hearts and pat dry.

3. Arrange artichoke quarters on the surface of the dough. Follow with mushrooms, Parmesan, mozzarella, green onion, and pepper. Drizzle with olive oil. Slide pizza onto heated baking stone and bake until well browned and puffy, about 20 to 25 minutes. Cut into small squares or wedges and serve hot.

Makes 12 to 15 cocktail wedges or 20 to 24 small squares.

PROSCIUTTO AND PEPPER PIZZA

This pie is ablaze with Italian color: the red of the peppers, the white of the cheese, and a spangle of fresh green parsley. Present it on a rustic wooden cutting board with a shaker of hot pepper flakes.

> Pizza Dough (see page 72)
> 5 ounces prosciutto, thinly sliced
> Sautéed Red Peppers (see page 36)
> ½ cup grated whole-milk mozzarella cheese
> ½ cup freshly grated Parmesan cheese
> ¼ cup minced parsley
> Olive oil

1. Preheat baking stone at least 30 minutes in a 450° F oven (475° F for a crisper crust). Roll pizza dough into a square or round and place on a well-floured inverted baking sheet.

2. Arrange whole slices of prosciutto on the surface of the dough. Top with peppers, including some of their cooking oil. Cover with mozzarella, Parmesan, and parsley. Drizzle surface with olive oil.

3. Slide pizza onto heated baking stone and bake until well browned and puffy, about 20 to 25 minutes. Cut into small squares or wedges and serve hot.

Makes 12 to 15 cocktail wedges or 20 to 24 small squares.

PIZZA MARGHERITA

The popular Italian salad of vine-ripened tomatoes with mozzarella and basil is "borrowed" here as a pizza topping. You can substitute strips of sun-dried tomato for some (but not all) of the fresh tomatoes, provolone cheese for the mozzarella, asiago or romano for all or part of the Parmesan. The one requirement is fresh, height-of-summer tomatoes.

> Pizza Dough (see page 72)
> 3 tomatoes, peeled, seeded, and chopped
> 1 cup grated whole-milk mozzarella cheese
> ½ cup whole fresh basil leaves
> Salt and black pepper to taste
> ¼ cup plus 2 tablespoons olive oil
> Freshly grated Parmesan cheese
> Pinch chopped fresh oregano

1. Preheat baking stone at least 30 minutes in a 450° F oven (475° F for a crisper crust). Roll pizza dough into a square or round and place on a well-floured inverted baking sheet.

2. Cover surface of pizza evenly with tomatoes, then cheese, then basil. Season with salt and pepper. Drizzle with ¼ cup olive oil, then dust with Parmesan and oregano. Slide pizza onto heated baking stone and bake until well browned and puffy, about 20 to 25 minutes. Brush crust with remaining 2 tablespoons olive oil. Cut into small squares or wedges and serve hot.

Makes 12 to 15 cocktail wedges or 20 to 24 small squares.

PISSALADIÈRE

All over the French Riviera, from the narrow alleys of old Nice to the beachfront cafes, you find "the pizza of Nice": *pissaladière*. Baked in large sheets and cut into squares while still warm, it's handed to you on a fragile tissue to munch as you go.

Cut into much smaller squares, it makes a fragrant before-dinner nibble, to offer with white wine and plenty of napkins. Its pungent olive-and-anchovy garnish piques the appetite and brings the Riviera a little closer.

Dough

½ package (1½ teaspoons) active dry yeast
¼ cup warm water (about 105° F)
½ teaspoon sugar
1¼ cups flour
½ teaspoon salt
½ teaspoon olive oil

Topping

Olive oil
¼ cup unsalted butter
4 yellow onions, thinly sliced
3 cloves garlic, minced
1 teaspoon minced fresh thyme or ½ teaspoon dried
Salt and black pepper to taste
1 tin (2 oz) anchovy fillets in oil
12 to 15 large black Greek olives, pitted
¼ cup minced parsley
¼ cup fresh basil leaves (optional)

1. *To prepare the dough:* In a small bowl combine yeast, water, and sugar and let proof 5 minutes. In large bowl of electric mixer, combine flour and salt. Using dough hook, begin mixing and add olive oil. Add yeast mixture and continue mixing. The dough hook will "knead" the dough for you. Mix 5 to 7 minutes, or until dough is silky and no longer clings to sides of bowl. *To make by hand,* put flour and salt in a large bowl and stir in olive oil and yeast mixture by hand; knead by hand on a lightly floured surface until mixture is silky and smooth. Place dough in a well-oiled bowl, turning to coat all surfaces with oil, and let rise, covered with a warm damp towel, for 1 hour.

2. *To prepare the filling:* In a large heavy skillet over medium heat, heat olive oil and butter. Add onion and cook gently for 5 minutes. Add garlic, thyme, salt, and pepper. Cook 20 minutes, or until onions are very soft but not brown. Taste; adjust seasoning if necessary. Put 2 anchovy fillets and half the olives in a blender. Add a few drops olive oil and blend. Add more oil as necessary to make a smooth paste.

3. *To assemble pissaladière:* Preheat oven to 400° F. Roll dough out into a rectangle or circle. Transfer to a well-floured inverted baking sheet. Spread with anchovy and olive paste and cover with onion slices. Arrange remaining anchovies over onions in a crisscross pattern. Slice remaining olives; arrange between anchovies. Drizzle with a little olive oil and dust with 2 tablespoons each parsley and basil (if used). Bake until well browned, about 30 to 35 minutes. Cool slightly, then sprinkle with remaining herbs just before serving. Cut while still warm.

Makes 16 to 20 small cocktail squares or wedges.

The sunny flavors of southern France come together in Pissaladière, the earthy "street" pizza from Nice. Anchovies, garlic, and olives are the soul of pissaladière, at its best in casual settings and washed down with a sharp white wine.

Sweet onions and pancetta—Italian bacon—are the savory topping for this Focaccia, a centuries-old, hearth-baked bread from Italy. A hot home oven can replace the hearth with good results.

SICILIAN PIZZA SOUFFLÉ

In the *tavernas* of Donalugata, Sicily, this puffy cheese pizza is called a "pizza soufflé." The poetic license is justified, for the topping does puff up and brown slightly, resulting in a most unusual *pizza bianco* (tomato-less pizza). No addition could possibly improve it. For best flavor, use good Italian Gorgonzola and whole-milk ricotta. Serve with a simple Italian red wine like a Valpolicella or Grignolino.

> Pizza Dough (see page 72)
> 1½ cups whole-milk ricotta cheese
> 4 ounces Gorgonzola cheese, crumbled
> 3 eggs
> ½ cup plus 2 tablespoons minced parsley
> 2 cloves garlic, minced
> 1 cup freshly grated Parmesan cheese
> Olive oil

1. Preheat baking stone at least 30 minutes in a 450° F oven (or in a 475° F oven for a crisper crust). Roll pizza dough into a square or round and place on a well-floured inverted baking sheet.

2. In a large mixing bowl, combine ricotta, Gorgonzola, eggs, ½ cup of the parsley, garlic, and half of the Parmesan. Spread this mixture over the surface of the dough. Drizzle with olive oil and dust with remaining Parmesan.

3. Slide pizza onto heated baking stone and bake until browned and puffy, about 20 to 25 minutes. Cut into small squares or wedges and serve hot, garnished with remaining parsley.

Makes 12 to 15 cocktail wedges or 20 to 24 small squares.

FOCACCIA

Out-of-town visitors to San Francisco's Italian neighborhood, North Beach, are likely to be puzzled by the thick, flat squares they spot in the bakeries and small markets. Some are brushed with tomato sauce and scallions, others with coarse salt and olive oil, still others with raisins and sugar. It's not pizza—or is it? No, it's *focaccia*, the original hearth-baked bread, still baked in the heart of North Beach by one of the city's oldest Italian families. If you buy it at the source, they will cut the large sheets into small rectangles, wrap them in butcher paper, and tie up the package with string. Chinese schoolchildren stop by in the morning for focaccia to slip into their satchels for a midmorning snack.

Cut into much smaller squares, focaccia makes marvelous cocktail fare. It can be baked before guests arrive, then cut up just when you need it. Best of all, it lends itself well to improvisation. Anything you can put on a pizza you can put on focaccia, although simplicity is a virtue here as elsewhere.

FOCACCIA WITH ONIONS AND PANCETTA

Crisp bits of *pancetta* (Italian unsmoked bacon) and sweet melted onions make a smooth, rustic topping for focaccia. Give it bite with freshly ground black pepper, and serve it with a lean, dry white Italian wine.

Dough

- 2 packages active dry yeast
- ½ cup warm water (about 105° F)
- 3 cups flour
- 1 cup warm milk

Topping

- ¼ cup olive oil
- ½ pound pancetta or bacon, thinly sliced
- 2 medium sweet red onions, thinly sliced
- 1 tablespoon sugar
- ¼ cup freshly grated Parmesan cheese
- Freshly ground black pepper

1. *To prepare the dough:* Dissolve yeast in warm water and let proof 5 minutes. Put 1 cup flour in a bowl and slowly incorporate the yeast mixture. Beat well, cover with plastic wrap, and set in a warm place for 1 hour. When dough has risen, stir in remaining 2 cups flour, then slowly incorporate the warm milk. Beat well, then cover again and let rise in a warm place for 45 minutes.

2. *To prepare the topping:* In a heavy skillet, heat olive oil. Add pancetta and render until crisp; drain on paper towels and crumble. In fat remaining in skillet, cook onions slowly, about 30 minutes, until they are "melted" but not brown. Add sugar and continue cooking until onions are quite soft and somewhat caramelized. Remove from heat.

3. *To assemble focaccia:* Preheat oven to 400° F. Oil a baking sheet well and pour in the dough—it will be rather soupy. Arrange onions and pancetta on top of the dough. Dust with cheese and pepper. Bake until well browned, about 35 minutes. Remove from pan; cool at least 10 minutes before cutting and serving.

Makes 16 to 20 small cocktail squares.

FOCACCIA WITH SWEET GARLIC PEARLS

A spoonful of garlic purée goes into the dough, with more sliced garlic strewn on top. This is garlic bread at its most glorious, to enjoy with Beaujolais, a light Côtes-du-Rhône, or a Valpolicella.

Dough

- 2 packages active dry yeast
- ½ cup warm water (about 105° F)
- 3 cups flour
- 1 cup warm milk

Topping

- ¼ cup olive oil
- 1 dozen cloves garlic, peeled
- ½ cup California Chablis or other slightly sweet white wine
- ¼ cup freshly grated Parmesan cheese
- ½ cup finely minced parsley
- Freshly ground black pepper

1. *To prepare the dough:* Dissolve yeast in water and let proof 5 minutes. Put 1 cup flour in a bowl and slowly incorporate the yeast mixture. Beat well; cover with plastic wrap and set aside in a warm place for 1 hour. When dough has risen, stir in mashed garlic (see topping directions below) and remaining 2 cups flour, then slowly incorporate the warm milk. Beat well, cover again, and let rise in a warm place for 45 minutes.

2. *To prepare the topping:* In a small saucepan heat olive oil. Add garlic and cook over moderately high heat for 5 minutes. Reduce flame to low and add wine. Cook garlic "pearls" gently for 30 minutes, or until most of the wine has evaporated and the garlic is very soft. You may have to add a little more wine depending on the age of the garlic. Remove pan from heat and reserve 6 garlic cloves. Mash remaining cloves with a spoon. Incorporate mashed garlic into dough.

3. *To assemble focaccia:* Preheat oven to 400° F. Oil a baking sheet well and pour in the dough—it will be rather soupy. Slice the reserved garlic; sprinkle over the dough. Dust surface with cheese, parsley, and pepper. Bake until well browned, about 35 minutes. Remove from pan; cool at least 10 minutes before cutting and serving.

Makes 16 to 20 small cocktail squares.

Party time calls for a tempting array of food—here, fresh shrimp, bouchées (a variation on the recipe on page 92), and flavored almonds.

menus for Entertaining

This chapter offers a dozen menus for all kinds of entertaining, as well as some guidelines for the Big Event. Although a party doesn't need to have a "theme," it can be a useful planning tool. A theme—even if it goes unannounced—helps you set a mood and coordinate a menu. Each of the following menus is based on a theme, with several hors d'oeuvre recipes plus suggestions for dishes to round out the menu. But a memorable party should bear the stamp of the giver, so use the following ideas as prompters for your own.

Ring in the New Year with friends, Champagne, and crab-topped toast, sweet-potato pancakes, bouchées, and oysters (see page 92).

Menu

NEW YEAR'S EVE COCKTAILS FOR 12

Hallie's Creamed Crab*

_Tea-Smoked Shrimp
(see page 42)_

Bouchées Dijonnaises*

_Cabbage Tourte
(see page 79)_

_Oysters and Their
Mignonettes*_

Sweet-Potato Galettes*

To keep your gathering going into the wee hours, don't play all your cards at once. Instead, bring out a series of dependable show-stoppers one at a time. Your guests will welcome the continuing parade of delights. Have a well-stocked self-service bar (see page 17) and chill a half-case of Champagne in the refrigerator. Recipes for the starred dishes follow.

HALLIE'S CREAMED CRAB

Crème de cassis is the secret of this dish's flavor. Tiny sake cups, available in Japanese markets or in most good houseware shops, make amusing serving pieces for the crab. You only need a dozen or so; just wash and dry them rapidly and refill them for the "second shift."

> 2 cups whipping cream
> ¼ cup dry vermouth
> 1 tablespoon crème de cassis
> Salt and pepper to taste
> 1 pound fresh crabmeat, picked over well to remove bits of cartilage
> 48 Toasted Bread Rounds (see page 30) or 12 ovenproof sake cups
> ¼ cup freshly grated Parmesan cheese
> Minced parsley or chives, for garnish

1. In a large saucepan combine cream, vermouth, and liqueur. Bring to a boil over high heat and reduce by half. Add salt and pepper; cool slightly. Stir in crabmeat.

2. Preheat broiler. Divide mixture among Toasted Bread Rounds or sake cups. Dust with Parmesan and broil just until cheese browns. Garnish with parsley and serve immediately.

Makes 4 dozen portions.

BOUCHÉES DIJONNAISES

A bubbling tomato-and-cheese mixture spiked with mustard fills these flaky mouthfuls—a sort of Welsh rarebit in a French wrap.

> _Quick and Easy Puff Pastry (see page 73)_
> 1 cup grated Gruyère cheese
> 1½ pounds ripe tomatoes, peeled, seeded, and chopped
> ¼ cup Dijon mustard
> Olive oil

1. Make bouchées as directed in step 1 of Creamy Mushroom and Liver Bouchées (see page 82). When bouchées are cool, remove the lids and scoop out the soft centers.

2. Preheat oven to 375° F. Place 1 teaspoon Gruyère in the bottom of each bouchée. Combine tomatoes and mustard and place a rounded teaspoon of tomato mixture in each bouchée. Top with a little more cheese and drizzle lightly with olive oil. Bake until cheese melts and tomatoes are hot throughout. Serve immediately from a silver platter.

Makes 15 bouchées.

OYSTERS AND THEIR MIGNONETTES

In France, raw oysters are often served with a mignonette—a peppery shallot and vinegar sauce. Here's the classic version along with several simple and delicious permutations.

> 5 dozen oysters, shucked and arranged on the half shell

The Basic Mignonette

> 1 tablespoon finely minced shallot
> 3 tablespoons Champagne vinegar
> 1 tablespoon cracked black peppercorns

Serve oysters on the half shell with the Basic Mignonette and several variations.

The Basic Mignonette In a small bowl whisk together shallot, vinegar, and pepper. Let rest 20 minutes before using. Makes about ¼ cup, or enough for 12 oysters.

Cilantro Mignonette Add 1 tablespoon minced cilantro.

Chile Mignonette Add finely minced jalapeño or serrano chile to taste.

Tomato Mignonette Add 2 tablespoons peeled, seeded, and chopped tomato.

Sweet Pepper Mignonette Add 2 tablespoons finely minced red, green, and/or yellow bell peppers.

SWEET-POTATO GALETTES WITH CRÈME FRAÎCHE

Potato pancakes with a twist: grated sweet potatoes and carrots are added to the russets. Serve from a silver platter with Champagne or vodka.

- 1½ cups grated russet potatoes
- 1½ cups grated sweet potatoes
- 2 tablespoons salt
- 1 cup grated carrot
- 5 eggs, lightly beaten
- ½ cup flour
- 1½ teaspoons salt
- 2 tablespoons lemon juice
- ¼ cup minced red onion
- 2 tablespoons minced parsley
- 2 tablespoons minced green onion
- 2 tablespoons minced chives
- 1 tablespoon minced garlic
  Pinch cayenne pepper
  Approximately ½ cup butter for frying
- 2 cups crème fraîche (see Note) mixed with ¼ cup minced chives and lightly salted

1. Combine potatoes in a colander; toss with the 2 tablespoons salt and let stand 30 minutes. Rinse, drain well, and pat thoroughly dry with kitchen towels.

2. In a large bowl combine potatoes, carrot, eggs, flour, the 1½ teaspoons salt, lemon juice, red onion, parsley, green onion, chives, garlic, and cayenne. Let mixture rest 20 minutes.

3. In a large skillet over medium heat, melt enough butter to thoroughly coat bottom. Drop in batter by large tablespoons and fry until well browned on both sides, about 3 minutes per side. Transfer to paper towels to drain briefly, then serve immediately with a large bowl of the crème fraîche mixture.

Makes 3 dozen small cocktail galettes.

Note If necessary, sour cream can be substituted for the crème fraîche.

Menu

MIDNIGHT SUPPER

Torta di Mascarpone*

Swiss Chard Tart With Pine Nuts*

Roast Balsamic Onions With Fontina*

Toasted Focaccia Fingers With Salami and Sun-Dried Tomatoes*

Onion Soup, Italian Style

Tuscan Country Bread

Warm Zabaglione Custard With Simmered Pears

Serve this simple Italian supper after the theater, the symphony, or the ball game. You can make the torta, the skewered onions, the focaccia, and the tart shell and filling before you leave. Once home, pop the tart and the focaccia in the oven; the focaccia will be ready in 10 minutes, the tart shortly thereafter. For Onion Soup Italian Style, substitute Marsala for Cognac in your favorite onion soup recipe and top it with grated Fontina instead of Gruyère; you might also add a few chopped porcini, if they're available. A Soave and a simple Chianti would make suitable wines. Recipes for the starred dishes follow.

TORTA DI MASCARPONE

This unctuous cheese torta is the creation of Peck's of Milan, the world-renowned fine food store. They send a little to this country, but you can easily make it yourself. *Mascarpone* is a fresh, light cheese similar to cream cheese but richer, available in fine cheese shops. If you can't locate mascarpone, you can come close to its buttery richness by blending cream cheese and butter. Layered with provolone, fresh pesto, and pine nuts, the torta is a handsome sight. It will slice best if cut immediately, then allowed to warm to room temperature, but you can also put it on a buffet whole and let your guests cut it themselves.

- ½ pound mascarpone or ½ pound softened cream cheese blended with 2 tablespoons softened butter
- ½ cup Pesto (see page 112)
- 1 pound provolone, sliced thin
- ½ cup pine nuts

1. Blend mascarpone and Pesto with a wooden spoon. On a serving platter, arrange a thin layer of provolone into a rectangle about 6 inches by 3 inches. Top with a ¼-inch layer of mascarpone-pesto mixture and a sprinkling of pine nuts. Repeat until all ingredients are used, ending with a layer of mascarpone-pesto mixture and a final sprinkling of pine nuts.

2. Chill torta in refrigerator several hours or until quite firm. To serve, cut in thin slices with a knife.

Serves 10.

SWISS CHARD TART WITH PINE NUTS

It's a Swiss chard tart, but not *just* Swiss chard; apples, cheddar, and pine nuts add three more dimensions. The filling is bound with just enough egg to hold it together, then baked in a flaky crust and served in warm wedges. The chard filling can be made up to six hours in advance.

> *Pâte Brisée (see page 72)*
> 1 cup chopped, cooked Swiss chard
> ½ cup grated Pippin apple, or other tart green apple
> ¼ cup toasted pine nuts
> ½ cup grated sharp Cheddar cheese
> 2 tablespoons Dijon mustard
> 1 tablespoon lemon juice
> Grated rind of 1 lemon
> Salt and pepper to taste
> Butter
> 1 egg mixed with 1 tablespoon whipping cream
> 2 tablespoons grated Parmesan cheese

1. Preheat oven to 375° F. Roll out Pâte Brisée ⅛ inch thick and transfer to a 9-inch tart tin. Prick the bottom of the shell well with a fork; bake 10 minutes. Cool tart shell slightly before filling.

2. In a bowl combine chard, apple, pine nuts, Cheddar, mustard, lemon juice, lemon rind, and salt and pepper. Transfer mixture to prebaked pie shell; dot the top with butter and drizzle the egg mixture over all. Dust top with Parmesan and bake until shell is well browned and top is firm, about 20 minutes. Cool slightly before cutting into wedges.

Makes 8 to 10 cocktail wedges.

ROAST BALSAMIC ONIONS WITH FONTINA

Tiny pearl onions turn sweet and soft when roasted with oil and vinegar, especially a vinegar as mellow and rich as Italian balsamic. The onions can be roasted a couple of days ahead; the cheese can be cubed and wrapped in plastic a day in advance. Paired on a cocktail skewer, they prove an especially happy marriage. The cheese will cube better if cold, but be sure to serve both cheese and onions at room temperature.

> 1½ pounds pearl onions
> ⅓ cup olive oil
> ¼ cup balsamic vinegar
> Salt and pepper to taste
> ¾ pound Italian fontina cheese, cut into ⅓-inch cubes

1. Preheat oven to 375° F. Blanch onions in boiling salted water 30 seconds. Drain. Slice off the root end. You should now be able to "peel" the onions easily by pressing them slightly between your fingers until the inner part slips out of the papery outer skin.

2. Whisk together oil, vinegar, and salt and pepper. Put onions in a roasting pan, add oil-vinegar mixture, and toss to coat well. Bake until tender, about 25 minutes. Remove from oven and let cool in pan. Taste; adjust seasoning as necessary. To serve, place 2 onions and 1 cheese cube on each cocktail skewer.

Makes 24 to 30 skewers.

TOASTED FOCACCIA FINGERS WITH SALAMI AND SUN-DRIED TOMATOES

Could anything be easier? Just buy good Italian salami and a jar of Italian *pumate* (sun-dried tomatoes), then layer them on your own home-made Focaccia. Heat and serve. Delicious!

> *Focaccia Dough (see page 87)*
> 6 ounces dry salami, sliced paper-thin
> 3½ ounces sun-dried tomatoes, in thin strips
> ¼ cup grated Parmesan cheese
> Olive oil

1. Preheat oven to 400° F. Oil a baking sheet well and pour in the dough. It will be rather soupy. Bake until well browned, about 25 minutes.

2. Reduce oven to 375° F. Cover focaccia with salami slices, overlapping them as necessary. Scatter sun-dried-tomato strips over the salami; dust with Parmesan and drizzle with olive oil. Reheat focaccia until Parmesan is browned and top is crusty. Cut into 2½-inch by 1-inch strips and serve piping hot.

Serves 12.

An Italian-inspired menu—Swiss chard tart, focaccia, roast onions, and cheese torta—makes an inviting, quickly assembled Midnight Supper.

Invite a crowd in for Gravlax With Dill Crêpes, open-faced Danish sandwiches, and a warming glass of aquavit. Recipes start on page 98.

menu

A SCANDINAVIAN SPREAD

Pickled Herring Platter

Gravlax With Dill Crêpes*

Smorrebrod*

Small Swedish Meatballs

Peppered Aquavit

Hot Spiced Wine

The fiery snap of aquavit—a clear distilled spirit flavored principally with caraway—is the perfect complement to the richness of herring and cured salmon, and to the hearty midday spread known as smorrebrod. A colorful "Cold Table" can make a memorable late-night supper, pre-theater buffet, or après-ski collation, especially with the addition of tiny, hot Swedish meatballs. Recipes for the starred dishes follow.

GRAVLAX WITH DILL CRÊPES

Salt- and sugar-cured salmon is a notable Swedish contribution to gastronomy and a traditional presence on a well-set *smörgåsbord*. The same curing technique works on sea bass and halibut too. It's usually served with mustard-dill sauce and a cucumber salad; but for an hors d'oeuvre, try it thinly sliced atop quartered Dill Crêpes or buttered Home-Style Danish Pumpernickel (see right). Note that you'll have to start at least a day and a half ahead to cure the fish.

    3 pounds fresh salmon fillet,
       skinned and boned
    1½ tablespoons sugar
    5 tablespoons kosher salt
    1 tablespoon vodka or aquavit
    7 tablespoons coarsely chopped
       fresh dill
       Grated rind of 2 lemons
    4 shallots, minced
       Additional vodka or aquavit
       Olive oil
       Lemon juice
       Freshly ground black pepper

Dill Crêpes

    Basic Crêpe Batter (see
    page 22)
    2 tablespoons finely minced
    fresh dill

1. Place salmon fillet on a sheet of plastic wrap or aluminum foil. Sprinkle with sugar, salt, and vodka. Cover tightly with plastic wrap or foil and refrigerate 1 day.

2. Put shallots in a small saucepan and add vodka to barely cover. Bring to a boil over high heat and cook until all the liquid has evaporated. Set aside to cool.

3. Unwrap salmon and sprinkle fillets with shallot mixture, dill, and lemon rind. Rewrap and place package on a rimmed cookie sheet with a 3- to 5-pound weight on top. Refrigerate at least 12 hours or up to 3 days.

4. To serve, slice gravlax thinly on the diagonal with a long, sharp knife. Arrange slices atop Dill Crêpes and garnish with a drizzle of olive oil, a squeeze of lemon, and some freshly ground black pepper.

Serves 15.

Dill Crêpes Add dill to Basic Crêpe Batter. Make crêpes as directed on page 22, but make them only 2 inches in diameter. Cool before stacking. Serve at room temperature.

HOME-STYLE DANISH PUMPERNICKEL

Here's a dark, dense loaf, moist and chewy, to use for buttered sweet onion sandwiches or a variety of Danish *smorrebrod* (see opposite page). It owes its distinctive flavor and texture to dark beer and mashed potatoes. Make it a day ahead for best flavor.

    2 tablespoons honey
    2 tablespoons molasses
       Grated rind of 1 orange
    2 tablespoons dark brown
       sugar
    2 tablespoons butter, melted
       and cooled
    2 cups water, preferably potato-
       cooking liquid
    ½ cup flat dark beer
    ½ cup coarsely ground cornmeal
       (polenta)
    2 packages active dry yeast
    1 cup cool mashed potatoes
    1 tablespoon salt
    2 cups rye flour
    1 cup stone-ground whole wheat
       flour
    4 cups unbleached flour
    1 egg beaten with 1 tablespoon
       whipping cream

1. In a large bowl stir together honey, molasses, orange rind, brown sugar, and butter. Scald the water and beer; pour over honey mixture. Gradually stir in cornmeal. Let mixture stand until lukewarm (about 110° F).

2. Sprinkle yeast over mixture and let proof 5 to 6 minutes. Beat in mashed potatoes and salt, then begin adding the flours, a cup at a time, stirring well after each addition. Turn dough out on a lightly floured surface and knead well for 5 minutes. Let rest 30 minutes.

3. Punch dough down (it will not have risen very much). Knead again, either with a dough hook or by hand, for 15 minutes. Transfer dough to a buttered bowl, cover with a damp towel, and let rise in a warm place until doubled in bulk, about 1½ hours.

4. Punch dough down and form into a large, round loaf. Transfer to a baking sheet sprinkled with cornmeal. Cover with a damp towel and let rise in a warm place until doubled in bulk, about 1 hour.

5. Preheat oven to 375° F. Brush dough with egg-cream glaze and let glaze dry. Brush again and bake bread until loaf sounds hollow when tapped on bottom, about 40 minutes. Cool on a rack before slicing.

Makes 1 large loaf.

SMORREBROD
The Danish tea sandwich

Literally "buttered bread," the word *smorrebrod* actually refers to a whole collection—an endless collection—of open-faced Danish sandwiches. The Danes eat them for lunch, but half-portions make splendid hors d'oeuvres. Let your good taste guide you; start with the suggestions listed below, then use your imagination to create a variety of dainty and colorful sandwiches. Use a sharp serrated knife to cut thin slices of Home-Style Danish Pumpernickel (preferably day-old). Spread the slices lightly with softened unsalted butter or seasoned butter to keep the bread from getting soggy. Garnish with a neat hand and an artful eye, making the sandwiches as colorful and tantalizing as you can. Eight or ten different choices is not too many; arrange them on a large tray or on a wooden cutting board.

☐ Thin-sliced pumpernickel, sweet butter, smoked trout.

☐ Thin-sliced pumpernickel, hazelnut butter, smoked turkey.

☐ Thin-sliced pumpernickel, horseradish butter, Applewood-Smoked Beef (see page 55).

☐ Thin-sliced pumpernickel, creamed herring, sliced red onion.

☐ Thin-sliced pumpernickel, salted butter, paper-thin slices of sweet red onion, capers.

☐ Thin-sliced pumpernickel, horseradish butter, sliced cucumber, sliced hard-boiled egg.

☐ Thin-sliced pumpernickel, butter, sliced Havarti cheese, thin-sliced radish, caraway seeds.

☐ Thin-sliced pumpernickel, butter, baby shrimp, lemon slice.

☐ Thin-sliced pumpernickel, currant jelly, and paper-thin slices of cold pork loin.

menu

GREEK EASTER LUNCHEON

*Grilled Shrimp
With Tomatoes, Garlic,
and Fennel**

Stuffed Grape Leaves*

Greek Olive Relish*

*Spinach and Feta
"Snake"**

Artichokes à la Grecque

Crown Roast of Lamb

*Rice Pilaf With Currants
and Pine Nuts*

*Herb Chutney With Yogurt
(see page 68)*

Fresh Grapes

Honey Pastries

Greek Coffee and Brandy

The traditional Greek Easter dishes could well grace any Easter table or serve as a menu for a spring dinner party. The crown roast can make a striking entrance, its center cavity mounded high with rice pilaf. Recipes for the starred dishes follow.

Traditional Greek Easter favorites include grilled shrimp, a spinach-stuffed filo "snake," an olive relish, and stuffed grape leaves.

GRILLED SHRIMP WITH TOMATOES, GARLIC, AND FENNEL

Marinating imbues these shrimp with garlic and fennel; careful broiling or grilling leaves them firm but moist. Either set the grilled skewers on Toasted Bread Rounds spread with Anchoiade, or serve the shrimp and bread rounds side by side. The anchovy, tomato, and shrimp make a delicious *ménage à trois*. If you use wooden skewers, soak them overnight to prevent their burning.

- ¼ cup olive oil
- ¼ cup lemon juice
- Grated rind of 1 lemon
- 2 tablespoons crushed fennel seed
- 1 tablespoon minced garlic
- Salt and pepper to taste
- 3 pounds jumbo shrimp, shelled and deveined
- 30 cherry tomatoes
- Additional lemon juice
- Toasted Bread Rounds (see page 30)
- Anchoiade (see page 38)

1. In a large bowl whisk together olive oil, lemon juice, lemon rind, fennel seed, garlic, and salt and pepper. Stir in shrimp, cover, and marinate in the refrigerator for 3 to 4 hours, or overnight.

2. Preheat broiler or prepare a charcoal fire. Thread each of 30 skewers with a shrimp, a cherry tomato, and another shrimp. Broil or grill until shrimp are bright pink and fairly firm; do not overcook. Sprinkle with a little more salt and pepper and brush with a little lemon juice. Pile skewers on a platter and serve with Toasted Bread Rounds spread with Anchoiade.

Serves 12 to 15.

STUFFED GRAPE LEAVES

Fresh mint, plenty of garlic, and a little feta cheese enliven these classic Greek *dolmas*. If you like, you can make them up to one week ahead and refrigerate them in their cooking liquid. Bring to room temperature before serving.

- 1 jar (1 lb) grape leaves preserved in brine
- ¼ cup olive oil
- 1 tablespoon butter
- ⅓ cup minced shallot
- 2 tablespoons minced garlic
- 3 cups cooked rice
- ¼ cup dried currants
- 2 tablespoons golden raisins
- ¼ cup chopped fresh mint
- ¼ cup finely minced parsley
- 1 teaspoon chopped fresh dill
- 2 ounces crumbled feta cheese
- Salt, pepper, and lemon juice to taste
- 3 to 4 cups hot chicken stock
- Greek Cucumber Sauce With Spinach and Dill (see page 38)
- Lemon wedges

1. Preheat oven to 350° F. Blanch grape leaves in boiling water 45 seconds to remove the briny flavor; drain and refresh under cold running water. Drain well and pat dry.

2. In a small skillet heat oil and butter. Add shallots and garlic and sauté over moderate heat until soft and slightly colored. Transfer to a large mixing bowl and add rice, currants, raisins, mint, parsley, dill, feta, salt, pepper, and lemon juice. Toss well with a fork to blend.

3. Lay a grape leaf out flat; put about 1½ tablespoons filling near the base of each leaf. Roll leaf into a cigar-shaped package, tucking in the sides as you roll. Repeat with remaining leaves. Transfer leaves to a roasting pan large enough to hold them snugly. Cover with stock and poach in the oven, covered, for 20 minutes. Cool in stock. To serve, mound grape leaves on a platter and accompany with Greek Cucumber Sauce With Spinach and Dill and a bowl of lemon wedges.

Serves 15 to 20.

GREEK OLIVE RELISH

This sassy relish has dozens of uses: Spread it on toast or crusty bread as an hors d'oeuvre; toss with hot pasta; serve with grilled lamb, tuna, or swordfish; spread on ham sandwiches; or tuck into pita bread along with grilled lamb. It can be made a week in advance; store in a covered jar in the refrigerator, with a "float" of oil on top.

- 1 pound imported black olives, preferably Greek Kalamata, pitted and finely chopped
- 1 cup green pimiento-stuffed olives, finely chopped
- ½ cup diced red bell pepper
- ¼ cup minced parsley
- 2 tablespoons minced garlic
- 3 tablespoons finely minced anchovy fillets
- 2 tablespoons minced fresh oregano
- ½ cup olive oil
- Freshly ground black pepper to taste
- Toasted Bread Rounds (see page 30)

In a large bowl combine black and green olives, red pepper, parsley, garlic, anchovy, oregano, olive oil, and black pepper. Cover and marinate overnight in the refrigerator. Serve with Toasted Bread Rounds or toasted pita-bread triangles.

Makes about 3 cups.

SPINACH AND FETA "SNAKE"

In the traditional Moroccan dish, stacked sheets of buttered filo are spread with almond paste, rolled up like a rope, then twisted into a coil. Here's a savory adaptation, featuring spinach and two kinds of cheeses. The finished "serpent" never fails to draw a crowd.

- ¼ cup olive oil
- ½ cup minced onion
- ½ pound crumbled feta cheese
- 2 eggs, lightly beaten
- 1 cup cooked chopped spinach, well drained
- ⅓ cup ground walnuts
- ½ cup ricotta or baker's cheese
  Salt and pepper to taste
- ½ pound filo dough
- 2 cups melted butter

1. Preheat oven to 375° F. In a small skillet over moderate heat, heat oil. Add onions and sauté until softened but not browned, about 5 to 6 minutes. Cool slightly.

2. In a bowl combine cooled onions, feta, eggs, spinach, walnuts, ricotta, salt, and pepper. Stir well with a fork to blend.

3. Layer three sheets of filo dough, brushing each sheet generously with melted butter. Using a third of the filling, and working from the edge of the filo closest to you, spread a strip about 1½ inches wide the length of the top sheet. Roll sheets into one long cylinder. Coil cylinder into a snake shape and place on a baking sheet. Repeat twice, coiling the second snake around the first, and the third snake around the second. Coils should be closely spaced but not touching. Brush with remaining butter and bake until golden, about 25 minutes, basting occasionally with butter that drips onto the baking sheet. Cool slightly, then cut into 1-inch chunks to serve, or let guests cut their own chunks off the "snake."

Serves 15.

Menu

A GARDEN WEDDING

New-Crop Asparagus Bundles*

Baked Prawns in Filo*

Baby Brioches With Onion Soufflé*

Baskets of Berries*

Grilled Loin of Spring Lamb Stuffed With Sorrel

Pilaf of Mixed Rices, Bulgur, and Kasha

Lemon Ice Cream

Wedding Cake

A wedding luncheon in a flower-filled garden is the dream of many a bride, and it's the perfect occasion to show off the bounty of spring. Here, verdant asparagus and baskets of berries reflect the springtime palette. Offer Champagne with the appetizers; pair a Cabernet Sauvignon with the lamb. Recipes for the starred dishes follow.

NEW-CROP ASPARAGUS BUNDLES

The pencil-thin, new-crop asparagus hardly need blanching, although a quick hot bath will bring out the best in them. They can be blanched, cooled, and dried several hours ahead. Keep them refrigerated, covered with a damp towel. To serve, tie them in bundles with green-onion "strings" and surround with an assortment of dipping sauces.

- 5 dozen pencil-thin, new-crop asparagus spears
- 2 bunches green onions
  Watercress Dip With Green Onions and Basil (see page 39)
  Curry Sauce (see page 39)
  Hot and Spicy Chinese Dipping Sauce (see page 38)

1. Bring a large pot of salted water to a boil and blanch asparagus 30 seconds. Drain, reserving water, and transfer asparagus to ice water to stop the cooking. Drain and pat thoroughly dry.

2. Trim green onion ends and peel away the tough outer skin. Bring reserved asparagus-blanching water to a boil again; blanch green onions 30 seconds, just to wilt. Drain, refresh under cold running water, and pat thoroughly dry.

3. With a small, sharp knife, cut 20 green-onion strips about 3 inches long and ⅛ inch wide. Arrange the asparagus in "bundles" of three, tying each bundle together with a strip of green onion. Arrange bundles on a platter and surround with dipping sauces.

Makes 20 bundles.

BAKED PRAWNS IN FILO

Storebought filo makes these pastries a snap. You simply marinate the prawns overnight in a zippy blend of olive oil, herbs, and lime, then wrap them in buttery filo and bake until crisp. A dipping sauce is optional.

> 5 *pounds raw prawns (approximately 12 to a pound)*
> ½ *cup olive oil*
> ⅓ *cup fresh lime juice*
> *Grated rind of 2 limes*
> ¼ *cup minced fresh herbs (any combination of parsley, chives, tarragon, and oregano)*
> 1 *tablespoon tomato paste*
> *Salt and pepper*
> 5 *sheets filo dough, cut into 6-inch squares*
> ¼ *cup melted butter*
> *Warm Parsley Sauce (see page 50) or Homemade Cocktail Sauce (see page 51) or Best-Ever Remoulade (see page 50), optional*

1. Shell prawns; devein if desired. In a large bowl whisk together olive oil, lime juice, lime rind, herbs, tomato paste, and salt and pepper to taste. Add prawns, stir to coat well, then cover and marinate, refrigerated, overnight.

2. Preheat oven to 375° F. Transfer prawns to a plate, shaking off excess marinade. Brush one filo square with melted butter; top with a second square and butter it, too. Place a prawn in the center of the square, then fold up the square like an envelope. Repeat with remaining filo and prawns. Transfer "packages" to a baking sheet and bake until golden, about 5 to 8 minutes. Serve hot with one or more of the dipping sauces, if desired.

Serves 20.

BABY BRIOCHES WITH ONION SOUFFLÉ

These tiny soufflés in brioche "cups" will charm all takers. A bit of oniony fluff in a warm, toasty brioche—who could resist?

> *Quick and Easy Brioche Dough (see page 74)*
> ¼ *pound bacon*
> 3 *cups minced onion*
> 3 *eggs, separated*
> ½ *cup whipping cream*
> ½ *cup sour cream*
> 2 *tablespoons brandy*
> *Salt, pepper, and ground nutmeg to taste*

1. Make 24 two-inch brioches according to instructions on page 74. Remove from tins and cool on a rack. When brioches are cool, scoop out the insides, leaving a sturdy wall, and reserve crumbs for another use. (They are excellent for stuffings, for meat loaves, or for topping casseroles.)

2. Preheat oven to 375° F. Cut bacon crosswise into ¼-inch widths. In a frying pan over moderate heat, render bacon pieces until they are crisp. Remove bacon with a slotted spoon to paper towels to drain. Pour off all but ¼ cup of bacon fat.

3. In the same frying pan over moderately low heat, fry onions in the bacon fat, stirring often, until they are soft and transparent but not browned. Transfer to a bowl, add the rendered bacon, and cool slightly. Add the egg yolks, cream, sour cream, and brandy. Add salt, pepper, and nutmeg to taste.

4. Whip egg whites with a pinch of salt until stiff but not dry. Carefully fold whites into onion mixture. Put a dollop of the soufflé mixture in the hollow of each brioche, set the brioches on a baking sheet, and bake until soufflés puff and brown, about 8 to 12 minutes. Serve immediately.

Serves 12.

BASKETS OF BERRIES

Buy the best, ripest berries you can find, pile them in baskets, and set the baskets all around the yard, with bowls of cool dipping sauce alongside. Berries with stems can be eaten as is; string the others on cocktail picks for easy dipping.

> *Strawberries*
> *Raspberries*
> *Blueberries*
> *Blackberries*

Grand Marnier Sauce

> 2 *cups sour cream or crème fraîche*
> 2 *tablespoons dark brown sugar*
> 2 *tablespoons Grand Marnier, or more to taste*
> *Grated rind of 1 orange*

1. Wash and pick over the berries; arrange attractively in baskets.

2. Make Grand Marnier Sauce and serve in bowls with berries.

Serves about 10.

Grand Marnier Sauce In a small bowl, whisk together sour cream, brown sugar, Grand Marnier, and orange rind.

An elegant garden wedding reception features asparagus, prawns baked in filo, brioches, and berries with a rich dipping sauce (see page 102).

menu

ITALIAN ANTIPASTO BUFFET

Sicilian-Style Olives (see page 15)

Prosciutto and Red Peppers (see page 36)

Marinated Squid (see page 40)

Porcini Tartlets*

Zucchini Gratin*

Braised Fava Beans alla Maria Zacco*

Caponata Pizza*

It's all "finger food"—to set out on a sideboard or a large buffet where your guests can help themselves. And it can all be done ahead, except for baking the porcini tartlets and the pizza. Italian food suggests Italian wine: Have a crisp, casual white like a Frascati or a Soave, and a fresh and fruity red, such as a Chianti or a Bardolino. Recipes for the starred dishes follow.

106

PORCINI TARTLETS

The fragrant porcini, also known as *cèpe* or *Boletus edulis,* is among the most prized of the wild mushrooms. It adds a rich, woodsy flavor to the mushroom filling and is well worth the added expense. Look for porcini in fine food markets. You can make the filling and the tart shells several hours in advance, then fill and bake shortly before serving.

> *Pâte Brisée (see page 72)*
> 1 ounce dried porcini mushrooms
> 1 pound white button mushrooms, stemmed, cleaned, and chopped
> 1 egg
> ¼ cup olive oil
> 2 teaspoons minced garlic
> 3 tablespoons peeled, seeded, and chopped tomato
> ¼ cup minced Italian parsley
> ¼ pound grated mozzarella cheese
> Salt and pepper to taste
> 3 tablespoons grated Parmesan cheese
> Additional minced Italian parsley, for garnish

1. Preheat oven to 375° F. Use Pâte Brisée to line 24 two-inch tart tins. Refrigerate while making the filling.

2. Soak porcini in warm water to barely cover for 20 minutes. With a slotted spoon, lift porcini out of soaking liquid. Strain liquid through a fine sieve to remove grit. In a small saucepan combine porcini and strained soaking liquid and cook over high heat until liquid has completely evaporated. Transfer porcini to a small bowl; stir in chopped button mushrooms and egg.

3. In a small skillet over moderate heat, heat 2 tablespoons of the oil. Add garlic and sauté until fragrant. Add the tomatoes and cook, stirring, until tomatoes just begin to release their moisture, about 5 minutes. Add to mushroom mixture.

4. Add parsley, mozzarella, and salt and pepper to mushroom mixture. Divide filling among tartlet shells, dust each with Parmesan, drizzle with remaining 2 tablespoons oil, and bake until hot throughout, about 12 to 15 minutes. Cool slightly before serving, garnished with parsley.

Makes 2 dozen tartlets.

ZUCCHINI GRATIN

You can bake this rich and custardy cheese casserole several hours ahead, then reheat it for serving. Cut it into squares and serve warm, with plenty of napkins.

> 1½ pounds zucchini, or enough to make 4 cups, grated
> ½ cup flour
> ¼ cup each grated mozzarella, fontina, Gruyère, and Parmesan cheese
> 2 tablespoons chopped fresh basil
> 4 eggs, lightly beaten
> Salt and pepper to taste
> Olive oil

1. Preheat oven to 375° F. In a large bowl combine zucchini, flour, cheeses, basil, eggs, and salt and pepper.

2. Press mixture into a buttered 11- by 15-inch baking dish. Bake until surface is firm and browned, about 25 to 30 minutes.

3. Remove from oven, drizzle top with olive oil, and place dish under a preheated broiler for a minute or two to brown the top well. Cool slightly, then cut into 36 squares and serve.

Serves 12.

BRAISED FAVA BEANS ALLA MARIA ZACCO

A Sicilian specialty from a very special Sicilian cook, these well-seasoned beans make delightful hors d'oeuvres when wrapped up in cool lettuce cups. On other occasions, serve them with a roast leg of lamb, pan-fried pork chops, or a baked ham. Note that the beans need to soak overnight.

> 1 pound dried fava beans
> 1 cup chopped yellow onion
> 3 tomatoes, coarsely chopped
> ½ cup tomato purée
> ½ cup coarsely chopped Italian parsley
> ½ cup coarsely chopped celery
> Salt and pepper to taste
> Dried hot red pepper flakes (optional)
> Lettuce cups
> Olive oil
> Parsley sprigs
> 4 ounces Parmesan cheese, sliced paper-thin

1. Put beans in a large pot; add water to cover and soak overnight. The next day, add onions, tomatoes, and tomato purée. Bring to a boil, reduce heat to maintain a simmer, and cook until beans are just tender. There should be almost no water left.

2. Cool beans to room temperature, then add parsley, celery, salt, pepper, and hot pepper flakes to taste, if desired. Serve beans in lettuce cups, garnished with a drizzle of olive oil, a parsley sprig, and a slice of Parmesan cheese.

Serves 12.

CAPONATA PIZZA

The Sicilians turn eggplant into a tangy, sweet-and-sour relish called *caponata*. Commonly eaten as antipasto, with good bread to soak up the juices, it also makes an uncommonly tasty pizza topping. There are as many versions of caponata as there are cooks; this particular rendition was inspired by San Francisco chef Joyce Goldstein.

> Pizza Dough (see page 72)
> 1 eggplant, about 1 pound
> ½ cup olive oil
> 2 onions, thinly sliced
> ½ cup celery, sliced ¼ inch thick
> ½ cup tomato purée
> ¼ cup minced garlic
> 2 tablespoons pine nuts
> 2 tablespoons sugar
> ¼ cup red wine vinegar
> Salt and pepper to taste
> ½ cup minced parsley
> ½ cup chopped black olives
> Additional olive oil
> ½ cup grated Parmesan cheese

1. Preheat baking stone (see page 83) at least 30 minutes in a 450° F oven (or, for a crisper crust, set oven at 475° F). Cut eggplant into ³⁄₄-inch cubes. In a large sauté pan over moderately high heat, heat 4 tablespoons of the olive oil. When oil is almost smoking, add half the eggplant cubes and sauté until they are lightly browned and softened. Transfer eggplant to paper towels. In the same pan, heat remaining 4 tablespoons oil; add remaining eggplant cubes and sauté until they are lightly browned and softened. Transfer to paper towels.

2. In the same skillet over moderate heat, sauté onions until soft but not browned, adding more oil if necessary. Add celery, tomato purée, and garlic; simmer 10 minutes.

3. In a small skillet over low heat, toast pine nuts, shaking pan constantly, until fragrant and lightly browned. Add toasted pine nuts to tomato mixture along with sugar, vinegar, salt and pepper, and parsley. Add eggplant and simmer 15 minutes. Remove from heat and stir in olives.

4. Roll pizza dough into a square or round and place on a well-floured upside-down baking sheet. Top with eggplant mixture, spreading it out evenly. Drizzle topping with a little more olive oil; sprinkle with Parmesan. Slide pizza onto heated baking stone and bake until well browned and puffy, about 20 minutes. Cut into small squares or wedges and serve hot.

Serves 12.

A hearty Italian antipasto buffet invites guests to help themselves to Caponata Pizza, Zucchini Gratin, Porcini Tartlets, and Braised Fava Beans (see page 106).

A SUMMER HARVEST SPREAD

Grilled Sweet Corn*

Cherry Tomatoes in Oil and Vinegar*

Grilled Vegetable Skewers With Smithfield Ham*

Zucchini-and-Corn Cakes With Pesto*

All-You-Can-Eat Steamed Clams

Drawn Butter and Crusty Bread

Field Greens Salad With Toasted Almonds

Raspberries in Cream

The splendid height-of-summer harvest provides plenty of party inspiration. Set up long picnic tables, chill some crisp California white wines and American beer, and call your party for the late afternoon when it starts to cool off. Enjoying summer's bounty in the setting sun is a fine way to salute the season. Recipes for the starred dishes follow.

GRILLED SWEET CORN

A charcoal fire and very fresh sweet corn are musts for this summertime delight. Another requirement: plenty of napkins! If you use wooden skewers, soak them overnight to prevent their burning.

> 12 *ears fresh-picked sweet corn*
> ½ *pound salted butter, melted*
> 2 *tablespoons olive oil*
> ¼ *cup minced fresh herbs (any combination of chives, parsley, thyme, and oregano)*

1. Prepare a medium-hot charcoal fire. Shuck corn and cut each ear into thirds. Bring about 4 quarts water to a boil, add corn, and cook 1 to 2 minutes (the fresher it is, the less it needs to cook). Drain corn well and thread one piece lengthwise onto each of 36 skewers.

2. In a small bowl, combine butter, olive oil, and herbs. Grill corn on all sides until slightly charred and smoky. Remove skewers to a serving platter, drizzle with herbed butter mixture, and serve immediately.

Makes 3 dozen skewers.

CHERRY TOMATOES IN OIL AND VINEGAR

Serve only sweet, vine-ripened tomatoes. If they're homegrown, leave the stems on; otherwise serve with cocktail picks. Note that the garlic and oil need to sit overnight.

> 1 *tablespoon minced garlic*
> ¼ *cup good-quality fruity olive oil*
> 2 *to 3 tablespoons balsamic vinegar, to taste*
> 2 *pounds cherry tomatoes*
>   *Kosher salt*
>   *Freshly ground black pepper*
> 1 *tablespoon julienned fresh basil*

1. In a small bowl marinate garlic in olive oil overnight. Add vinegar and whisk together well.

2. Put tomatoes in a bowl, add vinegar-and-oil mixture, toss to coat well, and let marinate at room temperature for 30 minutes. Sprinkle tomatoes with salt and pepper and garnish with basil.

Serves 10.

GRILLED VEGETABLE SKEWERS WITH SMITHFIELD HAM

The salty, smoky Smithfield ham from Virginia makes a delicious counterpoint to these grilled summer vegetables, but you can substitute prosciutto or any good, thin-sliced country ham. If you use wooden skewers, soak them in water overnight to prevent their burning. This can be plate-and-fork food, or guests can wrap a slice of ham around the hot grilled vegetables and eat with their fingers.

> 6 *small Japanese eggplants, cut in half lengthwise*
> 6 *small zucchini, cut in half lengthwise*
> 12 *cherry tomatoes*
> 12 *small carrots, cut into ¼-inch-thick slices*
> 1 *red bell pepper, cut into 2-inch cubes*
> 6 *ounces Smithfield ham, sliced paper-thin*
>   *Warm Parsley Sauce (see page 50)*

1. Prepare a medium-hot charcoal fire. Thread one half-eggplant lengthwise on each of 12 skewers; thread one half-zucchini lengthwise on each of 12 skewers. On a third set of 12 skewers, thread a cherry tomato, a carrot slice, and a red pepper cube. Grill the vegetables until they are slightly charred and smoky; they should be slightly softened but still crunchy.

2. Line a serving platter with a bed of ham slices. Arrange skewered vegetables on top and drizzle with Warm Parsley Sauce.

Serves 12.

*A charcoal grill makes summer
entertaining easy. Shown
here: grilled corn,
vegetable skewers, corn cakes,
and marinated cherry tomatoes.*

ZUCCHINI-AND-CORN CAKES WITH PESTO

These summery green-and-gold pancakes must be fried at the last minute, but the batter can be made a day ahead. Remove it from the refrigerator a half-hour before using. The pesto garnish can be made two or three days in advance, covered with a thin layer of olive oil, and stored in the refrigerator.

- 2 medium zucchini, grated
- 1 tablespoon coarse salt
  Corn Clouds (see page 76), completed through step 1

Pesto

- 2 cups loosely packed fresh basil leaves
- 1 cup olive oil
- 5 cloves garlic, minced
- 1 teaspoon salt
- 2 tablespoons toasted pine nuts
- 3 tablespoons butter, softened
- ¼ cup grated Parmesan cheese
- ¼ cup grated Romano cheese

1. Combine grated zucchini and salt. Transfer to a colander and let drain 1 hour. Pat dry.

2. Add zucchini to the Corn Clouds batter. Complete steps 2 and 3 of the Corn Clouds recipe. Garnish each cake with a teaspoon of Pesto. Serve immediately.

Serves 12.

Pesto In a food processor or blender, combine basil leaves, olive oil, garlic, salt, and pine nuts. Blend well. Transfer to a bowl and stir in butter, Parmesan, and Romano by hand.

A backyard with a pool, a summer house on the lake, or even a house with a large shaded terrace is an ideal setting for a Hawaiian party, featuring island dishes such as Lomi-Lomi, Polynesian Prawns, and roasted suckling pig. Keep it cool and casual, with a tub full of chilled beer and dry white wine and a ready pitcher of Planter's Punch (see page 15). If you don't have the yen to do it yourself, many delicatessens or caterers will cook a whole suckling pig for you. Recipes for the starred dishes follow.

LOMI-LOMI

Lomi-Lomi is a Hawaiian hors d'oeuvre, traditionally made with salted salmon. That's not easy to find on the mainland, but fresh salmon makes a reasonable substitute. If you wait to salt the dish until just before you serve it, you can make the lomi-lomi up to one day in advance.

- 1 pound salmon fillet, skinned and cut into ⅓-inch cubes
- 1 cucumber, peeled, seeded, and cut into ¼-inch dice
- 2 tomatoes, peeled, seeded, and cut into ¼-inch dice
- ½ cup minced red onion
- 2 green onions, minced
- ½ cup fresh lime juice
- 2 tablespoons olive oil
  Salt and freshly ground black pepper
- ⅓ cup minced cilantro
  Toasted Bread Rounds (see page 30), lettuce cups, or endive leaves
  Thinly sliced onion rings, for garnish

1. In a large stainless steel, ceramic, or glass bowl, combine salmon, cucumber, tomatoes, red and green onions, lime juice, and olive oil. Stir gently, cover with plastic wrap, and let marinate, refrigerated, for at least 1 hour or up to 24 hours.

2. Remove salmon from refrigerator a half-hour before serving. Season to taste with salt and pepper; stir in cilantro. Serve on Toasted Bread Rounds, in lettuce cups, or in endive leaves, garnishing with thinly sliced onion rings.

Serves 12.

SWEET-AND-SOUR PORK

You can alternate skewers of Polynesian Prawns and these spicy cubes of pork on a platter and serve the Plum Sauce as a partner to both. The pork is traditionally deep-fried, as described in step 2, but if you wish you can bake it instead, as described in step 3. Note that whichever cooking method you choose, the pork needs to marinate at least 3 hours.

- 2 tablespoons dark soy sauce
- 2 tablespoons brown sugar
- ¼ cup cider vinegar
- 2 tablespoons minced fresh ginger
- ½ cup minced green onion
- 1 dried hot red pepper, ground to a powder
- ½ teaspoon ground cumin
- ½ teaspoon ground anise seed
- 1 teaspoon salt
- 1½ pounds pork tenderloin, cut into ½-inch cubes
  Peanut oil for deep-frying (optional)
  Lemon wedges

1. In a large stainless steel, ceramic, or glass bowl, combine soy sauce, brown sugar, vinegar, ginger, ¼ cup of the minced green onions, chile-pepper powder, cumin, anise seed, and salt. Add pork and toss to coat well. Marinate, covered and refrigerated, for at least 3 hours or overnight.

2. *To deep-fry:* Heat 3 inches of oil in a deep skillet or deep-fryer to 375° F. Drain meat, reserving any marinade. Deep-fry meat until well browned, about 3 to 5 minutes. Drain briefly on paper towels, then arrange in a warm serving bowl. Garnish with remaining ¼ cup minced onion and serve immediately with lemon wedges and a bowl of toothpicks. Any reserved marinade can be drizzled over the top.

3. *To bake:* Preheat oven to 350° F. Transfer the pork and its marinade to a covered casserole and bake until tender, about 30 to 35 minutes. Check occasionally to make sure meat is not drying out, and add a little water if necessary.

Serves 12.

POLYNESIAN PRAWNS

A zesty sweet-and-sour plum sauce is the partner for these prawns. Serve with chilled beer—or Mai Tais for a Hawaiian island flavor.

- 3 pounds large prawns, boiled and shelled
- 2 tablespoons minced parsley
- 1 teaspoon grated lemon rind

Plum Sauce

- 2 pounds purple plums
- ¼ cup fresh lemon juice
- ½ cup red wine vinegar
- ¼ cup Japanese plum wine or sake
- 1 tablespoon Dijon mustard
  Cayenne pepper
  Salt

Arrange prawns on a serving platter. Combine parsley and lemon rind and sprinkle over prawns. Serve with Plum Sauce and cocktail picks.

Serves 10.

Plum Sauce Cut a cross in the bottom of each plum. Plunge into boiling water briefly, then into a bowl of ice water. Peel the plums (skins should peel off easily) and pit them. In a food processor or blender, combine plums and lemon juice and blend until smooth. Stir in vinegar, plum wine, and mustard. Add cayenne and salt to taste.

TROPICAL FRUITS WITH HAWAIIAN CREAM

Fresh tropical fruits make a refreshing hors d'oeuvre on a hot summer day. Serve them with the lightly sugared Hawaiian Cream as a dip. You can either set cocktail picks alongside, or skewer the fruit before you arrange it on the platter. A cool pitcher of Planter's Punch (see page 15) would almost seem *de rigueur.*

- 1 mango, peeled and cubed
- 1 papaya, peeled and cubed
- 1 pineapple, peeled, cored and cut into 1-inch cubes
- 2 bananas, peeled and cut into ¼-inch chunks
- 2 avocados, peeled and cubed
  Juice of 1 lemon
  Dried banana chips (optional)
  Toasted unsweetened coconut (optional)

Hawaiian Cream

- ½ cup crème fraîche or sour cream
- 2 tablespoons dark rum or coconut liqueur
- ¼ cup packaged sweetened grated coconut
- 1 tablespoon brown sugar, or more to taste
- 1 tablespoon lemon juice, or more to taste

Prepare fruits, sprinkling bananas and avocados with lemon juice to prevent discoloration. Arrange fruits in neat mounds on a serving platter, alternating them to best show off their colors. If desired, include dried banana chips and sprinkle the fruit with toasted coconut. Serve with Hawaiian Cream as a dip.

Serves 12.

Hawaiian Cream In a small bowl, combine crème fraîche, rum, coconut, brown sugar, and lemon juice. Taste; add more sugar or lemon juice if needed.

Makes 1 cup.

A Hawaiian Poolside Party calls for tropical fruits, Sweet-and-Sour Pork, prawns, Lomi-Lomi, and something cool and fruity to drink (see page 112).

Tex-Mex cooking has summer appeal all over the country. Let guests help themselves to the Tostaditas, Fiesta Platter (shown opposite), and Black Bean Dip, and pass onion rings (shown opposite) and Seviche. The dinner can be served as a buffet, or you can set platters of food, family-style, the length of the dinner table. Recipes for the starred dishes follow.

BEER-BATTER-FRIED ONION RINGS

This fluffy, light batter can also be used to coat Gulf shrimp, zucchini, chicken wings, or squid.

>   2 pounds sweet onions, sliced
>   ¼ inch thick
>   2 cups milk
>   2 cups flour
>   2 eggs, separated
>   2 cups dark beer
>   2 teaspoons salt
>   Peanut oil for deep-frying
>   Kosher salt

1. Soak onions in milk for 3 hours. Drain; discard milk, or save it for use in soups or corn muffins.

2. In a large bowl whisk together flour, egg yolks, beer, and salt. Beat egg whites until stiff but not dry; fold into beer batter.

3. Heat plenty of oil in a large, deep pot or deep-fryer to 375° F. Dip onion rings in batter; let extra batter drip off. Fry onion rings until golden, turning once with chopsticks or tongs; transfer to paper towels to drain briefly. Sprinkle lightly with salt and serve immediately.

Serves 12.

TOSTADITAS

Freshly fried homemade corn tortilla chips—better than any you'll ever buy! You'll want to make several batches to accompany the Fiesta Platter and the Black Bean Dip.

>   6 day-old corn tortillas
>   Corn oil for deep-frying
>   Kosher salt

Cut each tortilla into 6 wedges. In a large, deep pot or deep-fryer, heat plenty of corn oil to 375° F. Fry the tortilla wedges in small batches until golden. Using a slotted spoon, transfer to paper towels to drain. Sprinkle lightly with salt. Do not fry chips more than 4 to 5 hours in advance.

Makes 3 dozen chips.

BLACK BEAN DIP

You can use this delectable dip to fill enchiladas or burritos, to top tostadas, or to spoon inside soft or crisp tacos. Note that the beans need to soak overnight. The dip can be made two or three days in advance and stored in the refrigerator, but do not serve it cold; reheat it slowly, adding a little olive oil and warm water to thin it.

>   1 pound black beans
>   1 cup chopped onion
>   3 fresh jalapeño chiles
>   1½ tablespoons minced garlic
>   1½ teaspoons ground cumin
>   1 tablespoon freshly grated
>   orange rind
>   1 cup olive oil
>   ½ teaspoon annatto oil
>   (available in Hispanic
>   markets), optional
>   Kosher salt
>   1 hard-boiled egg, minced
>   ¼ cup minced green onion

1. Pick beans over to remove any dirt or pebbles. Put them in a large pot and add water to cover. Let soak overnight.

2. In a blender or food processor, combine onion, jalapeños, garlic, cumin, and orange rind. Blend well.

3. Drain beans and discard water. Return beans to pot and add fresh water to cover. Add ¼ cup of the olive oil, bring to a boil, reduce heat, and cook until tender, about 1 hour. Purée beans in blender or food processor.

4. In a large skillet heat remaining ¾ cup oil over moderate heat. Add onion purée and annatto oil (if used). Sauté about 5 minutes, stirring often; add bean purée and continue cooking 10 minutes. Season to taste with salt. Serve dip from skillet, if desired, or transfer to a serving bowl. Garnish top with minced egg and green onion. Serve warm or at room temperature with Tostaditas.

Makes about 6 cups.

FIESTA PLATTER

Use the Anaheim chiles if you prefer a milder version; the jalapeño chiles are for the fearless. Note that the beans need to soak overnight.

   1 *cup raw pinto beans*
  ½ *cup chopped onion*
  2 *cloves garlic, minced*
  1 *serrano chile, minced*
  1 *teaspoon ground cumin*
  ¼ *cup lard or vegetable shortening*
  3 *ripe avocados, coarsely mashed*
  3 *tablespoons yogurt*
  3 *tablespoons fresh lime juice*
     Salt
  1 *bunch cilantro, coarsely chopped*
  4 *green onions, chopped*
  4 *ounces peeled and chopped Anaheim chiles or 2 jalapeño chiles, minced*
  4 *ounces sharp Cheddar cheese, grated*
  4 *ounces Monterey jack cheese, grated*
15 *pitted black olives, chopped*
  1 *to 2 fresh tomatoes, seeded and chopped, but not peeled*
     Chili powder

1. Pick beans over to clean them, then soak overnight in water to cover. Drain, discarding liquid. Put beans in a heavy pot with 6 cups fresh water, the chopped onion, garlic, serrano chile, cumin, and lard. Bring to a boil, reduce heat to maintain a slow, steady simmer, cover, and cook until beans are tender, about 1½ hours, adding more water as necessary to keep mixture slightly soupy. Mash beans with a wooden spoon and spread them into a round on a 12-inch platter.

2. In a small bowl combine avocados, yogurt, lime juice, and salt to taste. Stir in half the chopped cilantro. Spread avocado mixture on top of the beans.

3. Sprinkle the avocado mixture with green onions, chiles, grated cheeses, olives, and tomatoes. Dust the top with chili powder and the remaining cilantro. Serve with plenty of Tostaditas.

Serves 12.

Gather friends around your car for a convivial tailgate warmup. Here, the spicy crab mixture fills several large artichokes instead of baby ones.

A PRE-GAME TAILGATE WARMUP

*Artichokes With
Spicy Crab**

*New Potatoes With Caviar**

*Walnut Gorgonzola Bites**

*Antipasto Skewers**

*Panbalie**

Lasagne

Garden Salad

Crusty Bread

*Homemade Fudge
Brownies*

*This menu can be
either a pre-game or
a post-game
collation, or, if you
prefer, serve the hors
d'oeuvres before
and save the rest for
later. Lasagne, well
wrapped in foil
and a bath towel
"cozy," will keep
warm for
several hours. Store
the salad in plastic
bags and dress
it just before serving.
Recipes for the
starred dishes follow.*

ARTICHOKES WITH SPICY CRAB

In this case, "spicy" does not mean hot; it means "well seasoned"—with mustard, green onions, capers, and more.

> 24 *baby artichokes*
> 1 *lemon*
> ¾ *pound fresh cooked crabmeat*
> ¼ *cup whipping cream*
> 1 *tablespoon capers*
> ¼ *cup finely chopped green pepper*
> 2 *tablespoons minced green onion*
> 2 *teaspoons Dijon mustard*
> 1 *tablespoon butter*
> 1 *teaspoon olive oil*
> 3 *tablespoons minced shallot*
> 2 *tablespoons white wine*
>   *Salt and pepper*
>   *Worcestershire sauce*
>   *Minced parsley*
>   *Lemon wedges*

1. Pull off dark green outer leaves of artichokes until you reach the pale green "heart." Cut ½ inch off top and trim stem end down to the pale green part. Rub artichoke hearts well with lemon and cook in boiling salted water until tender. Drain and pat dry. Pull out some of the innermost leaves and spread the hearts open slightly.

2. In a bowl combine crabmeat, cream, capers, green pepper, green onion, and mustard. In a small skillet over moderate heat, heat butter and oil. Add shallots and cook until translucent, about 4 to 5 minutes. Add wine and cook until mixture is reduced to a glaze. Cool slightly and add to crab mixture. Season to taste with salt, pepper, and Worcestershire sauce.

3. Stuff artichoke hearts with crab mixture. Pack into a tightly sealed container along with a plastic bag of minced parsley and the lemon wedges. At serving time, garnish hearts with minced parsley and serve with lemon wedges.

Serves 12.

NEW POTATOES WITH CAVIAR

Don't blanch: The caviar need not be expensive imported sturgeon roe (although it can be!). Let your budget be your guide in selecting from among the variety of colorful caviars on the market (see page 47), then pack them in ice for the trip. The contrast of warm potato with sour cream and ice-cold caviar makes a memorable mouthful. The foil will keep the potatoes warm for several hours, but you may want to pack them in an insulated carrier as well.

> 3 *dozen tiny red-skinned new potatoes*
>   *Olive oil*
>   *Kosher salt*
>   *Juice of 1 lemon*
> 12 *ounces assorted caviar (golden, red, and black)*
>   *Sour cream or crème fraîche*
>   *Lemon wedges*

1. Steam potatoes over boiling salted water until they are just tender when pierced. Dry them well; drizzle them while hot with olive oil, then sprinkle with salt and lemon juice. Cut off the top of each potato about ¼ inch down; scoop out and discard some of the inside pulp, leaving a firm, thick-sided shell. Wrap potatoes in foil and place in a tightly sealed container.

2. At serving time, set out potato "shells," caviars, sour cream, lemon wedges, some tiny serving spoons, and plenty of napkins. Guests can fill their potato "shells" with sour cream and the caviar of their choice, with a little lemon juice squeezed over the top.

Serves 12.

WALNUT GORGONZOLA BITES

While you're readying the rest of the hors d'oeuvres, pass these toasted walnut "bites."

72 perfect walnut halves
⅓ pound ripe Gorgonzola cheese, at room temperature
3 tablespoons unsalted butter, softened

1. Preheat oven to 350°F. Toast walnut halves on a cookie sheet until they are fragrant and lightly browned. Cool completely.

2. In a small bowl, work cheese and butter together with a wooden spoon. Sandwich two nut halves with a dab of the cheese mixture. Refrigerate briefly to firm the cheese. Serve cool but not cold.

Makes 3 dozen "bites."

ANTIPASTO SKEWERS

Olives and cheese, prosciutto and melon come together on these colorful skewers. It's an Antipasto Platter made into finger food, and it's open to dozens of variations: Shrimp, feta cheese, and Greek olives? Mozzarella, cherry tomatoes, and rolled anchovies? You decide.

1 large or *2 small seasonal melons, peeled and cut into 36 cubes*
½ pound prosciutto, sliced paper-thin
1 pound Italian fontina cheese, cut into 36 cubes
36 best-quality black olives
    Olive oil
    Freshly ground black pepper

1. Wrap each cube of melon in a piece of prosciutto.

2. On each of 36 skewers, thread a cube of cheese, an olive, and a prosciutto-melon cube. Place skewers in a tightly sealed container.

3. At serving time, drizzle with olive oil and dust with freshly ground black pepper.

Makes 3 dozen skewers.

PANBALIE

A juicy shrimp sandwich from the French Mediterranean, *panbalie* tastes better when the filling has had time to "marry" and soak into the bread. On game day, pack the sandwiches into your basket first and weight them down with the rest of the tailgate goodies. They'll be all the better for it! The shrimp mixture may be made a day ahead and stored in the refrigerator.

1 pound cooked tiny shrimp
2 red onions, coarsely chopped
¼ cup olive oil
3 tablespoons lemon juice
1 tablespoons minced fresh oregano
    Salt and pepper
6 six-inch, day-old French rolls
3 ripe tomatoes, thinly sliced

1. In a small bowl combine shrimp, onions, 2 tablespoons of the olive oil, lemon juice, oregano, and salt and pepper to taste.

2. Slice rolls in half lengthwise. Moisten each half with a little of the remaining olive oil. Arrange tomato slices on the bottom half. Spread shrimp mixture over tomato slices and add top half of roll. Wrap each sandwich tightly in foil. At serving time, slice each sandwich in halves or thirds.

Serves 12.

COME FOR SHERRY AND TAPAS

Garlic and Hot-Pepper Almonds (see page 14)

Olives Marinated With Orange and Fennel (see page 14)

Pumpkin Satchels (see page 76)

*Chorizo and Potato Tortilla**

*Shrimp in Sherry Almond Butter**

*Mushroom Tortilla**

*Fried Sausage in Cabbage Leaves**

Tapas *are Spanish cocktail nibbles, often provided by bars and cafes at no charge. Tapas and sherry make a pleasant switch from the usual cocktail party collation. Lay in an assortment of sherries, set the tapas around the room in small bowls, and put some classical guitar music on the stereo. Recipes for the starred dishes follow.*

Invite friends in for sherry and tapas, the Spanish version of the cocktail hour, with shrimp, a pair of Spanish tortillas, and fried sausage-and-cabbage rolls.

CHORIZO AND POTATO TORTILLA

The Spanish tortilla bears no resemblance to the more familiar Mexican one. It is actually a sort of open-faced omelet, akin to the Italian frittata, that can be served either hot from the skillet or at room temperature. In tapas bars, you may be offered a small plate with a few cubes of tortilla on it. The potato version is by far the most common, but a tortilla with shrimp, artichoke hearts, or asparagus tips would not be unusual.

- ¼ pound chorizo (smoked Spanish sausage, not the Mexican variety), cubed
  About 6 tablespoons olive oil
- ½ cup chopped white onion
- 1 cup cubed boiled potatoes (½-inch cubes)
- 4 eggs, lightly beaten
  Salt and cayenne pepper
  Minced parsley

1. In a small frying pan over moderate heat, fry the chorizo until it is hot throughout. With a slotted spoon, transfer to a large bowl.

2. Add enough of the oil to the frying pan to make 3 tablespoons. Add the chopped onion and sauté over moderate heat for 3 minutes. Add the potatoes and cook over moderately high heat until they are well browned. Add mixture to chorizo. Cool at least 5 minutes or up to 3 hours; do not refrigerate.

3. In a separate 8-inch skillet, heat 3 tablespoons of the olive oil over moderate heat until oil is almost smoking. Add eggs to chorizo mixture, season to taste with salt and cayenne, then pour the mixture into the hot skillet. Shake the skillet occasionally to keep the eggs from sticking to the bottom. When tortilla is firm on top but not dry, run a knife around the edge, shake the pan a little, cover the skillet with a plate, and invert. Then slide the tortilla back into the skillet to brown the other side. Transfer to a serving platter, sprinkle with parsley, and cut into wedges to serve.

Makes 8 small wedges.

SHRIMP IN SHERRY ALMOND BUTTER

The tangy, slightly salty quality of a good dry sherry flatters all kinds of shellfish, especially shrimp. These are best served hot from the oven with cocktail picks. If you can't bake all of them at once, do them in batches, dividing the butter, garlic, almonds, and sherry accordingly.

- ½ cup unsalted butter, at room temperature
- 2 tablespoons minced garlic
- ½ cup finely ground almonds
- ¼ cup dry Spanish sherry
- 3 pounds medium-sized raw shrimp, shelled
  Salt
  Minced parsley

1. Preheat oven to 350° F. Put butter, garlic, almonds, and sherry in a baking dish large enough to hold the shrimp. Place dish in oven and heat until butter melts and foams.

2. Add shrimp, stir to coat with mixture, and bake until shrimp turn pink and begin to curl, about 5 to 6 minutes. Transfer to a serving platter, pour any remaining sauce on top, salt lightly, and garnish with minced parsley. Serve immediately.

Serves 16.

MUSHROOM TORTILLA

Mushrooms and sherry are delightful together, as this mushroom tortilla proves. It is best served hot or slightly warm; you can make it a couple of hours ahead, but reheat it briefly in a warm oven.

- About 7 tablespoons olive oil
- 1 tablespoon minced garlic
- ½ cup minced white onion
- ½ cup minced red onion
- 3 cups diced mushrooms
  Salt and pepper
- 6 eggs, lightly beaten
- 1 tablespoon butter
  Minced parsley

1. In a large skillet over moderately low heat, heat 4 tablespoons of the oil. Add garlic and sauté until it is fragrant but not browned, about 5 minutes. Add onions and continue cooking for 10 minutes, adding a little more oil if mixture starts to stick to the skillet. Add mushrooms and cook until they just begin to exude their liquid. Remove from heat. Season to taste with salt and pepper. Let cool at least 5 minutes or up to 2 hours; do not refrigerate.

2. Add eggs to the mushroom mixture. In an 8-inch skillet over moderate heat, heat 3 tablespoons of the oil and 1 tablespoon butter. When oil is almost smoking, add egg mixture. Cover the pan and cook until tortilla is firm to the touch but not dry, shaking the skillet occasionally to keep the eggs from sticking to the bottom. Run a knife around the edge, shake the pan a little, cover the skillet with a plate, and invert. Slide the tortilla back into the skillet to brown the other side. Transfer to a serving platter, garnish with minced parsley, and cut into wedges to serve.

Makes 8 wedges.

FRIED SAUSAGE IN CABBAGE LEAVES

This Spanish "stuffed cabbage" is remarkably easy because it uses ready-made breakfast links. Serve the sausages hot from the skillet, with a crock of mustard if desired.

- 2 pounds mild breakfast link sausages
- 1 large green cabbage
- 16 cups salted water
- 2 eggs, lightly beaten
- ½ cup flour
  Vegetable oil, for frying
  Salt

1. Put sausages in a skillet with water to cover, bring to a boil, reduce heat to maintain a simmer, cover, and cook until sausages are almost cooked through but still slightly pink inside. Drain and set aside.

2. Core cabbage. In a large kettle bring the water to a boil. Add whole cabbage, reduce heat to a simmer, and blanch 10 minutes. Using a slotted spoon, remove cabbage to a colander to drain. When it is cool enough to handle, peel back the leaves one by one and lay them out on paper towels. Cut out the center rib of the larger leaves.

3. Wrap each sausage with a cabbage leaf, folding it up to create a neat package. Pat dry. Dip each package in beaten eggs, then in flour.

4. In a large, deep skillet, heat 1 inch of oil to 375° F. (Check temperature with a candy/deep-fry thermometer.) Add sausage packages in batches and fry until golden brown on all sides. Transfer to paper towels to drain. Slice packages on the diagonal, ½ inch thick. Salt lightly and serve piping hot.

Serves 16.

---

menu

FRENCH BISTRO HORS D'OEUVRES

Brandade Fritters*

Savory Clafouti*

Hallie's Walnut and Red-Onion Bread Rounds With Toasted Gruyère*

Brioches à l'Anchoiade*

Mediterranean Fish Soup

Rabbit in Mustard Sauce

Fresh Noodles

Endive Salad

Camembert

Hot Apple Tart

When the year's first Beaujolais (Beaujolais Nouveau) is released each November 15, it's meant to be drunk within 6 to 9 months. Celebrate its arrival with a tasting at home. Ask your wine merchant for several of the nine different Grand Cru villages to compare. These simple wines go best with casual food like the French country dishes in this "Bistro" menu. You can serve the hors d'oeuvres during the tasting (which wouldn't be done at a more serious tasting, but this one's all fun), then set the bottles on the table to drink with dinner. Recipes for the starred dishes follow.

BRANDADE FRITTERS

The creamy, garlicky salt-cod purée called brandade (see page 46) can be turned into creamy, garlicky fritters. The dough can—indeed should—be made in advance, but the crusty fritters must be fried at the last moment.

- 3 tablespoons butter
- ½ cup whipping cream
- ½ cup plus 3 tablespoons sifted flour
- 2 eggs
- 1 egg yolk
  Brandade (see page 46)
  Peanut oil for deep-frying

1. In a saucepan over low heat, heat butter and cream until butter melts and mixture just begins to simmer. Remove from heat and add flour all at once. Beat with a wooden spoon until flour is fully incorporated. Add eggs and egg yolk, one at a time, beating well after each addition. Beat in Brandade. Refrigerate for 1 hour.

2. Pour peanut oil into a large, deep skillet or deep-fryer to a depth of 3 inches. Heat oil to 375° F. Using a scant 2 tablespoons of brandade mixture per fritter, drop the batter into the oil in small batches and fry until the fritters puff up and brown. Drain on paper towels and serve immediately.

Makes about 3 dozen fritters.

123

Old French bistro dishes inspire new cocktail variations—Savory Clafouti, Brandade Fritters, and walnut bread with Gruyère (see page 123).

SAVORY CLAFOUTI

The traditional French *clafouti* is a simple, country-style fruit dessert, a cross between a custard and a pudding. The same principle produces a delectable savory, with spicy sausage and colorful peppers bound in a well-seasoned egg-and-cream custard.

- ½ pound spicy sausage meat
- 2 tablespoons butter
- 1 tablespoon olive oil
- ¼ cup each *minced red and yellow onions*
- 2 tablespoons dry white wine
- 2 tablespoons flour
- 1 cup whipping cream
- 4 eggs, lightly beaten
  Salt and pepper
- ½ cup thinly sliced bell peppers (red, yellow, or green)

1. Preheat oven to 350° F. In a skillet over moderate heat, sauté sausage until fully cooked. Drain the sausage and set aside.

2. In a separate large skillet, heat butter and oil over moderate heat. Add onions and sauté until translucent but not browned. Add wine and continue cooking 1 minute. Stir in flour and remove from heat.

3. Add cream and stir well to prevent lumps; mixture should thicken. Add sausage and eggs; season to taste with salt and pepper. Transfer mixture to a buttered 12- by 16-inch baking pan. Top with peppers and bake until bubbly and browned, about 20 to 25 minutes. Serve the clafouti hot, warm, or at room temperature. Cut into squares just before serving.

Serves 12 to 16.

HALLIE'S WALNUT AND RED-ONION BREAD ROUNDS WITH TOASTED GRUYÈRE

You can make the moist, nutty bread a day in advance; otherwise, start at least four hours before you need it to give it a chance to cool. Use only good-quality imported Gruyère for best results.

The Bread

- 1 package active dry yeast
- ⅓ cup warm water (105° F to 115° F)
- 3½ to 4 cups unbleached flour
- ½ cup whole wheat flour
- 1 tablespoon salt
- 1 cup warm milk (105° F to 115° F)
- 1 cup coarsely chopped walnuts
- ¾ cup finely chopped red onion
- ½ cup unsalted butter, softened
- 2 tablespoons cornmeal

The Topping

- ½ pound Gruyère cheese, coarsely grated
- ¼ cup whipping cream
  Salt and cayenne pepper

1. *To make the bread:* In a large bowl combine yeast and the warm water and let proof 5 minutes. Add 1¾ cups of the unbleached flour, the whole wheat flour, salt, and milk. Beat about 2 minutes. Add walnuts, onion, and butter; mix thoroughly. Beat in remaining flour ½ cup at a time to make a stiff dough. When dough becomes too stiff to stir, turn out onto a lightly floured surface. Knead gently until dough is smooth and elastic, about 10 minutes, incorporating more flour as necessary to keep dough from sticking. Transfer to a buttered bowl, turn to coat it with butter, cover with a towel, and let rise in a warm place until doubled in bulk, about 1 hour.

2. Preheat oven to 425° F. Punch dough down and knead gently on a lightly floured surface for 3 to 4 minutes. Shape into a long loaf and put on a baking sheet sprinkled with cornmeal. Let rise, uncovered, in a warm place for 15 minutes.

3. Place a pan of hot water on the oven floor or on a lower rack. Slash top of dough with scissors in three places and bake 30 minutes. Remove pan of water, reduce oven heat to 300° F, and bake until bread is well browned and sounds hollow when tapped on the bottom, about 30 more minutes. Cool on a rack. When bread is thoroughly cool, slice into rounds ¼ inch thick.

4. *To assemble the hors d'oeuvres:* Preheat oven to 375° F. In a bowl combine Gruyère, cream, and salt and cayenne pepper to taste. Divide cheese mixture among bread rounds, arrange rounds on a baking sheet, and bake until bubbly, about 10 to 12 minutes. Serve immediately.

Serves about 20.

BRIOCHES À L'ANCHOIADE

Tiny brioches cut in half make the most delicious "finger sandwiches," here filled with a Provençal anchovy spread and a thin sheet of Parmesan.

- 2 dozen 2-inch brioches (see page 74)
- 8 ounces aged Parmesan or Asiago cheese
  Anchoiade (see page 38)
  Olive oil
  Freshly ground black pepper
  Minced fresh thyme

Cut brioches in half, reserving tops. Using a cheese plane, slice Parmesan into paper-thin slices. Spread brioche bottoms with Anchoiade; top each with a slice of Parmesan. Drizzle with a little olive oil, sprinkle with freshly ground black pepper, and dust with minced thyme. Replace the brioche tops and serve.

Makes 2 dozen brioches.

INDEX

U.S. MEASURE AND METRIC MEASURE CONVERSION CHART

		Formulas for Exact Measures			Rounded Measures for Quick Reference		
	Symbol	**When you know:**	**Multiply by**	**To find:**			
Mass (Weight)	oz	ounces	28.35	grams	1 oz		= 30 g
	lb	pounds	0.45	kilograms	4 oz		= 115 g
	g	grams	0.035	ounces	8 oz		= 225 g
	kg	kilograms	2.2	pounds	16 oz	= 1 lb	= 450 g
					32 oz	= 2 lb	= 900 g
					36 oz	= 2¼ lb	= 1,000 g (1 kg)
Volume	tsp	teaspoons	5.0	milliliters	¼ tsp	= 1/24 oz	= 1 ml
	tbsp	tablespoons	15.0	milliliters	½ tsp	= 1/12 oz	= 2 ml
	fl oz	fluid ounces	29.57	milliliters	1 tsp	= 1/6 oz	= 5 ml
	c	cups	0.24	liters	1 tbsp	= ½ oz	= 15 ml
	pt	pints	0.47	liters	1 c	= 8 oz	= 250 ml
	qt	quarts	0.95	liters	2 c (1 pt)	= 16 oz	= 500 ml
	gal	gallons	3.785	liters	4 c (1 qt)	= 32 oz	= 1 l.
	ml	milliters	0.034	fluid ounces	4 qt (1 gal)	= 128 oz	= 3¾ l.
Length	in.	inches	2.54	centimeters	⅜ in.	= 1 cm	
	ft	feet	30.48	centimeters	1 in.	= 2.5 cm	
	yd	yards	0.9144	meters	2 in.	= 5 cm	
	mi	miles	1.609	kilometers	2½ in.	= 6.5 cm	
	km	kilometers	0.621	miles	12 in. (1 ft)	= 30 cm	
	m	meters	1.094	yards	1 yd	= 90 cm	
	cm	centimeters	0.39	inches	100 ft	= 30 m	
					1 mi	= 1.6 km	
Temperature	° F	Fahrenheit	5/9 (after subtracting 32)	Celsius	32° F	= 0° C	
					68 °F	= 20° C	
	° C	Celsius	9/5 (then add 32)	Fahrenheit	212° F	= 100° C	
Area	in.^{2}	square inches	6.452	square centimeters	1 in.^{2}	= 6.5 cm^2	
	ft^2	square feet	929.0	square centimeters	1 ft^2	= 930 cm^2	
	yd^2	square yards	8,361.0	square centimeters	1 yd^2	= 8,360 cm^2	
	a	acres	0.4047	hectares	1 a	= 4,050 m^2	

Acknowledgments

Calligraphy
Chuck Wertman
San Francisco, CA

Additional Photography
Michael Lamotte, back cover
Laurie Black, Academy photography

Photograph of Danielle Walker by Fischella

Additional Food Styling
Amy Nathan, back cover
Jeff Van Hanswyk, at The Academy

Editorial Assistance
Don Mosley

Copyediting
Linda Rageh

Proofreading
Andrew Alden

Color Separations
Color Tech Corp
Redwood City, CA

Special Thanks to:

Paul Bauer Fine China and Crystal
San Francisco, CA

Biordi Art Imports, Inc.
San Francisco, CA

J. Canes Antiques
San Francisco, CA

Family Tree Antiques
Oakland, CA

Forrest Jones, Inc.
San Francisco, CA

Bob Hartmann Studios
San Francisco, CA

La Ville du Soleil
San Francisco, CA

Leisure Pool and Patio
Oakland, CA

Scott Miller
Oakland, CA

Our House
San Francisco, CA

Palacek Imports
San Francisco, CA

People's Bazaar
Berkeley, CA

Jeanne Quan
Berkeley, CA

R. Escott Jones Designs
San Francisco, CA

Peter Tamano
Berkeley, CA

Maria and Carlo Zacco
Rome, Italy